The Must-React System

The Must-React System

User's Guide to Prospecting C-Suite Executives

Kraig Kleeman

iUniverse, Inc.
New York   Bloomington   Shanghai

The Must-React System
User's Guide to Prospecting C-Suite Executives

iUniverse books may be ordered through booksellers or by contacting:

iUniverse
1663 Liberty Drive
Bloomington, IN 47403
www.iuniverse.com
1-800-Authors (1-800-288-4677)

Because of the dynamic nature of the Internet, any Web addresses or links contained in this book may have changed since publication and may no longer be valid.

The views expressed in this work are solely those of the author and do not necessarily reflect the views of the publisher, and the publisher hereby disclaims any responsibility for them.

ISBN: 978-0-595-48942-8 (pbk)
ISBN: 978-0-595-62895-7 (cloth)
ISBN: 978-0-595-60902-4 (ebk)

Printed in the United States of America

For my mother and father:
Dad is the master of verbal communication.
Mom is the master nurturer.
I love and adore them both.

For an Old Friend

Still I Rise

You may write me down in history
With your bitter, twisted lies,
You may trod me in the very dirt
But still, like dust, I'll rise.

Does my sassiness upset you?
Why are you beset with gloom?
'Cause I walk like I've got oil wells
Pumping in my living room.

Did you want to see me broken?
Bowed head and lowered eyes?
Shoulders falling down like teardrops.
Weakened by my soulful cries.

Does my haughtiness offend you?
Don't you take it awful hard
'Cause I laugh like I've got gold mines
Diggin' in my own backyard.

You may shoot me with your words,
You may cut me with your eyes,
You may kill me with your hatefulness,
But still, like air, I'll rise.

Does my sexiness upset you?
Does it come as a surprise
That I dance like I've got diamonds
At the meeting of my thighs?

—Maya Angelou, 1978

Contents

Foreword

Kraig Kleeman is an amazing person. And *The Must-React System* works. At least, it did on Bono.

It had been a long, arduous week of airports, limos, meetings, and phone calls. Bono always enjoys warm summer nights in Amsterdam, but this particular night, he was simply worn out. He wanted three things prior to lights out and bedtime: (i) a hotel room, (ii) privacy, and (iii) a cold beverage. As he arrived at his hotel, Bono was disappointed to be notified by the attendant that the hotel was not offering room service this particular evening. He debated whether to order in from a neighboring restaurant or to send me (his traveling assistant) out for a pickup. After all, Leidseplein is one of Amsterdam's popular centers for nightlife with theaters, cafes, restaurants, cinemas, the casino, and more. Street musicians, jugglers, fire-eaters, and other performers make the square a lively place until the early hours, especially on a warm summer evening. Neither Bono nor I was tempted to enter into the nightlife, however. We were simply exhausted from the events of the week. Bono finally decided that visiting the lounge would be the quickest route to food and drink. We made our way to the lounge area of my posh hotel to get that coveted cold beverage, and to just "sit" for a few minutes alone. It was time for Bono to collect his thoughts from the events of both the week and day. Bono doesn't typically sit in public places alone. The truth is that it's not easy being the front man for rock band U2 and a variety of social awareness/ social change organizations. Maintaining privacy is an ongoing challenge. On this night, however, I reckon that Bono's appearance in public was destined to happen. Why? Because of Kraig Kleeman and the power of *The Must-React System*. Mr. Kleeman did what no other human being can do to Bono. He approached him during private time and gained an unsolicited forty-five-minute meeting. Little did Bono know that Kraig was an expert in the area of gaining meetings with executives and celebrities.

Here's what happened: I found a quiet seat for Bono in the corner of the hotel's main lounge. While sipping on a beverage, several fans attempted to approach him and ask the usual questions about his music. In order to maintain privacy, Bono often travels with at least one assistant and sometimes more than one, depending upon his schedule, the number of public appearances, etc. As much as he enjoys interacting with fans, he doesn't always have the time or energy to engage in the many requests for autographs and/or spontaneous dialogues. It's the sort of thing that just comes with the territory of being a public figure. Bono always attempts to strike a good balance between offering reasonable fan access and maintaining downtime when he needs it. On this particular night, Bono instructed me to run interference. That's a term we use that means "block out anyone who might approach him." The fact is that he was extremely worn down from a rigorous schedule. He wanted a cold beverage and a sandwich. And that was it. As usual, several people tried to approach him, but as his trusted assistant, I protected Bono's solace by politely and successfully intervening each time, per his instructions.

While sitting and relaxing, Bono heard a voice not far from where he was sitting shout, "Hey Bono!" As is natural, Bono looked in the direction from where he heard his name. He then locked eyes with an American man who stated, "I appreciate so much how you defend *the poor of the earth!*" Oh my! This American had Bono's undivided attention. *The poor of the earth* has become a very important, if not vital, phrase in his global humanitarian efforts. No one has ever approached him using that phrase. Bono's interest in this American had now piqued, simply because he used the very language that embodies his passion. The American went on to say, "I was formerly on the board of directors of an outreach to abandoned children in South America. I appreciate your efforts at getting the modern world to understand the pain and challenges that exist in the rest of the world. Cheers to you, Bono!" Wow. No one had ever approached Bono like that before. He is accustomed to people approaching him about his music, certain lyrics in a song, and things of this sort. But this man had Bono's attention immediately, because he approached Bono about what is core. What he values. What keeps me him up at night. What is central to his goals and purposes in life. Bono was hooked! He asked me (Bono's assistant) to invite this American man over to his area of the lounge. Kraig and Bono visited for nearly an hour, and they have maintained a friendship since. Little did Bono know that Kraig has developed a powerful selling system entitled *The Must-*

React System, and that he had utilized the principles of *Must-React* to lure him into a dialogue. I take my hat off to Kraig Kleeman! In a funny sort of way, I guess Bono was a target who succumbed to *The Must-React System*.

Aedon O'Reilly
Assistant to Bono

Preface

If you were to walk into my office today, you would notice several things. Apart from the normal administrative paraphernalia scattered about, you would probably gravitate toward one of the many drawings of rock legends on my wall. For example, my dear friend Bono is displayed prominently. Mick Jagger is featured in the center of one drawing with the rest of the Rolling Stones surrounding him. I love a great concert or a good record. Throughout this book, I will occasionally cite lyrics from popular songs. Hopefully they will provide more than just color. Rock lyrics become popular because they connect with the core of what is important to people. Some of the greats, like Jagger, have been able to connect to something that is almost universally true and totally essential to the human experience. That isn't just the key to a great rock song; it's also key to a successful career. Some people never grasp this essential concept. I, on the other hand, have exhibited a natural ability since my youth.

During my teen years, I spent much of my time listening to the rock legends of the day: Steve Miller Band, AC/DC, Ted Nugent, Alice Cooper, and others. If you were living in the St. Louis area at that time, you would have probably tuned in to KSLQ "Super Q" to listen to their Top 40 format during the week and celebrity DJ Lee Ford on Sunday nights. Mr. Ford's talk show, *Point Counterpoint,* was uncanny. He had a unique ability to consistently craft Sunday evening talking points that appealed to the teen crowd. Ford was half talk show host, half DJ, and an all around funny-guy. In short, he was a legend among my friends and I. Anyone who was able to get through the phone lines to participate with Ford gained immediate popularity in our group.

> It's a long way to the top,
> If you want to rock and roll!
>
> —AC/DC, 1982

A lot of area teenagers boasted about occasionally getting onto Ford's show. But I found more challenge in trying to make myself an "unofficial" member of the radio cast. With brute force tenacity, a handful of teenagers found their fifteen seconds of fame on *Point Counterpoint*. I certainly had a lot of brute force and tenacity on the telephone. But fifteen seconds of fame wasn't enough for me. I wanted to be a regular guest. They weren't exactly holding auditions, but my persistence and my techniques more than compensated. Week after week, I would call in to the show, work my way through the screening staff, and emerge on the airwaves with a smart quip, a joke, or a generally amusing conversation topic for Mr. Ford.

I began to develop a small cult following. People would call in just to ask about the mystery caller. And week after week I appeared, like clockwork, to the amusement of all my fans. For a young kid from the Midwest, I was hitting the big time, and I liked it.

Several years later, I began attending college at a small liberal arts college northwest of Chicago. I was extremely active in student life by serving as Student Senate president, president of College Republicans, chairman of Young Republicans for Kane County, a resident assistant in the dorm, and the leader of a variety of other committees and social events. I also dated Jodie Andersen, a stunningly attractive young woman who would be crowned homecoming queen the following year. Life was good in 1979!

I occasionally organized teams that would trek into urban Chicago with the goal of discovering new cultures and differing ways of life. Through the recommendation of a wise and caring professor, I was able to justify many of my road trips to urban Chicago as "academic" according to certain department policy, none of which I would understand without the coaching of Dr. Clossman. That meant reimbursement for gasoline, tolls, meals, and even the use of a college vehicle! On one such odyssey, I led a team of utterly suburban kids to spend the day in the heart of Chicago's south side at an Operation Push meeting. Everyone from our group looked forward to listening to Reverend Jesse Jackson articulate his branded speech, which was popular for mixing visceral cries for biblical faith along with his trademark roars concerning a plethora of social injustices.

Here I am, on the road again,
Here I go, playing star again,
There I go, turn the page.

—Bob Seger, 1973

But merely sitting in the pews and participating in Mr. Jackson's "amen corner" was not enough for me. So, prior to our trip, I had engaged some of Mr. Jackson's staff on the telephone. At this point in my life, I had not received any sales training. I wasn't at all connected with Jackson's staff; I was just a nineteen-year-old college kid from St Louis who was fearless on the telephone. With a "gut-level" ability to communicate and persuade, I organized an in-person lunch meeting with the reverend himself! My college professors were stunned when my group reported that we had enjoyed a private meal with one of Chicago's most prominent political activists. I remember the dean of students asking me, "Kraig, how did you achieve access to a lunch meeting with Jesse Jackson?" I would be queried many times in the years ahead about my ability to secure meetings with high-level executives almost on-demand. As a college student, I had not yet organized illustrative language and a principle-based description of *The Must-React System*. The reason I was able to secure minor celebrity as a teen and a meeting with Reverend Jesse Jackson was that I was a natural born cold-caller.

I have read what seems like hundreds of those sales manuals and strategies. I've gone to the seminars, and I've been briefed. So many times I wonder if these "experts" have ever picked up a phone or given a sales presentation, much less closed a deal. I realized early in my life that I had a skill that was crucial to sales success. I was able to get a hold of anybody on the phone. I didn't realize the power of that ability as a teen on the "Super Q" or as a young college student leader meeting with Jesse Jackson. But I have spent much of my professional career trying to draw principles and teachings out of my own experience to share with others. This natural God-given ability has been boiled down into a group of principles that I have labeled *The Must-React System*. It has been a blessing to me in both my professional and my personal life. My hope is that it is a blessing to you in yours.

Kraig Kleeman
CEO, Blaire Group

Introduction

There are two types of sales cycles: large, complex sales that involve a minimum of multiples of hundreds of thousands of dollars and that have elapsed time cycles of multiples of months, even years; and there are transactional sales that are lower-priced, and where the sales cycle is multiples of days, weeks, or sometimes even immediate—not months or years. While helpful for all selling environments, this book emphasizes *The Must-React System* as applied to complex, enterprise-class sales. My next book will analyze applying our methodology to transactional sales.

Prospecting is broken, especially for sales professionals who manage complex sales cycles. Salespeople throughout the country, regardless of industry, are just plain bad at devising strategies to meet new prospective customers and developing new relationships that lead to new closed business. This is especially true when the targeted buyers are senior-level, C-suite executives. I don't want to get into all the reasons why some feel more comfortable milking their existing accounts. Regardless of the reason, there is a great need for sales organizations to acquire new business. If companies can't prove to Wall Street that they are acquiring new accounts and increasing their customer base, they will suffer losses. It's as simple as that. And for that reason alone, CEOs will yell at sales executives, who in turn will yell at regional directors, who will yell at managers, all the way down the line to you. This book is all about gaining access to your targets.

While cold calling is one of the most important tools for prospecting, prospecting is not just about cold calling. It is a group of practices that are a part of demand creation within a company. It includes introductory messaging, cold calling, presentation delivery, e-mails, and a variety of campaigns, e.g., trade shows, webinars, direct mailings, etc. *The Must-React System* is a prospecting system. It is a methodology that creates meaningful activity, and it provides an entirely new approach to cold calling and e-mail campaigns. The principles of

Must-React should be applied to all aspects of your corporate prospecting strategy to achieve maximum results.

Every company that wants to continue growth needs its sales team to be proficient in finding and closing net-new opportunities. But, unfortunately, most salespersons are not good at gaining new business, much less performing even the most basic prospecting practices. There are a multitude of reasons for this phenomenon.

Let's examine the large-scale problem before we dig into specifics. Prospecting is not being addressed holistically. What I mean by that is you think there are different techniques for net new customers on the one hand and new opportunities with current customers on the other. Most companies think that cold calling, e-mailing, PowerPoint presentations, and trade shows are unrelated activities. There is disproportionate attention placed on pipeline with little attention paid to demand-creation processes. In reality, these are not separate areas, but they have been treated as such by a majority of companies. A holistic view of the sales pipeline incorporates demand creation into its strategy and objectives. Prospecting of any sort is all about creating sales opportunities or leads. Most companies do not have a clear practice of how these leads are received, qualified, approved, and managed as they develop into sales cycles.

For many executives, this information is intuitive. But, consider that Blaire Group has found that 69% of professional business-to-business (B2B) sales organizations fail to properly disseminate leads to field-sales or partner-sales organizations. This means that hard work is being done by part of your company to create demand, but it is not being developed by the appropriate groups to make sure that it bears fruit. Whether these are leads originated from trade shows that are compiled in the customer relationship management (CRM) system or from partners who are interested in joint activity, the delivery of leads is broken.

We have also discovered that a majority of companies do not have a clearly defined strategy for dealing with demand creation once it is delivered to the sales group. 81% of sales management executives do not track activity metrics that are consistent with best practices. If you are a sales manager, do you know if your reps have followed-up on leads generated from the most recent trade show your company attended? Do you know how many were called? Who declined a meeting? What were the reasons? Who was never actually contacted? Why? How many contacts decided to attend next-step meetings? What were their interests? Most of the companies I speak with cannot answer these simple questions about even their most important campaigns. We also know that 42% of organizations do not have adequate call-management systems in place. The management of lead development is broken.

And yet, 72% of all sales organizations are dissatisfied with both the quality and quantity of their sales pipelines. I have met very few leaders of sales organizations that feel they have an adequate pipeline developed. I repeat: prospecting is broken.

> Ain't no use jivin'
> Ain't no use jokin'
> Everything is broken
>
> —Bob Dylan, 1989

The problems with prospecting can't all be blamed on large-scale issues like a rift between sales and marketing or a lack of attention paid to the demand-creation process. There are a host of problems with the way sales and marketing professionals go about prospecting. Blaire Group has found that a majority of these professionals have similar, ineffective prospecting practices, such as:

- an inability to control the prospect/call,
- disorganized call-preparation activity,
- weak cold-calling skills,
- ineffective use of e-mail messaging,
- over-use of product-centric messaging,
- the inability to conduct executive-level briefings,
- and an untenable prospecting follow-up system.

These are all symptoms of broken prospecting. What are the causes? We know that there is a lack of training and a culture of resistance to current practices.

The first problem is that the salesperson is untrained in prospecting methods. Let's take cold calling as an example. Cold calling isn't intuitive for most people, even if they are great salespeople. I once knew a sales rep that sold several multi-million dollar products and was the number one rep in the company but never called a single new prospect. All of the work was done in old customer accounts, where he was well-known and well-liked. Great salesperson, lousy cold caller. I spent a few hours on the phone with him, and the reason was quickly apparent: he had no clue how to get into a company that didn't welcome him with open arms. I don't mean to say that this person wasn't a fantastic politician in his accounts. He was a wizard in account-management activities, for sure. But if he and others like him want to remain competitive in the years ahead, he needs to learn how to cold call.

Another rep I knew claimed to devote two days of his week to cold calling. On these two days, he claimed to make one hundred cold calls. A lot of people feel like they need to make high volumes of calls to get results. According to conventional wisdom, good results for direct marketing efforts, like cold calling, are typically less than 1%. That means, according to the so-called experts, if you made one hundred calls in a week, you'd be lucky to get one person to meet with you. There is no way to put that amount of effort into cold calling and still complete all of the other tasks you have in active sales cycles. But what I want to argue is that the reason for the poor results isn't that cold calling is an ineffective activity; it's that people are doing it badly. Let me be specific—most sales professionals do not understand how to cultivate quality "talk time" into their cold-calling activities. This means that although a lot of calls are being made, they are not generating meaningful dialogue with the prospect.

Many have failed so often at cold calling that they feel that their time is better spent on other efforts. "I'm really a closer and not a prospector," they often opine. But in reality, these salespeople are not good at generating new interest in accounts where they are well-established. They typically only sell to one or two departments, places where they have developed friendships due to the generosity of the American Express corporate card. These people are rarely good at plumbing the depths of their customer bases. They are afraid of hurting their existing contacts, so they become stuck in the few departments to which they have been introduced. The purpose for prospecting is not just getting new customers. It's also about developing new relationships in existing accounts. One company I worked for had released a successful product in the mid-1980s. Several years later, they re-branded the product under a different name. But more than a decade later, when I was hired to help prospecting efforts, they still had major accounts that had no idea any re-branding had ever occurred. It shouldn't take ten years to inform your current customers that you've changed the name of your product. But the reality of the situation is this: if you struggle to get new customers, you probably struggle to fully cover your current accounts.

It's no wonder people are so poorly trained at cold calling. The so-called "experts" are total phonies! I never cease to be amazed at the plethora of books, articles, lectures, and topical tidbits written about the topic. Many of these so-called "experts" have little to offer other than personality and charisma. None of them have the history of getting on-demand meetings like I do.

I have been in the sales consulting business for the past decade. I'm well aware of the different tactics and strategies that are proposed. I want to discuss a few of my "favorites" and talk about why they appeal to people and why they are totally useless.

Frank Rumbaska has a system titled "Never Cold Call Again!" In this manuscript, (which he basically gives away), he tries to say that since cold calling is difficult, abandon the activity altogether. You can see why this appeals to people. We already talked about how salespeople fail so often at cold calling. If someone tells you that the practice is doomed to failure, you start to think that it isn't your fault. This is the classic victimization cop-out. It might make your wounds feel better, but it won't find and close deals.

Rumbaska likes to point out a lot of the issues we've talked about so far. He proclaims that he's a better salesperson than most because he doesn't waste time cold calling. He contests that cold calling is statistically unproductive and needs to be avoided altogether.[1]

Give me a break. Just because Frank was as bad at cold calling as everybody else doesn't mean cold calling is dead. Frank might not make phone calls anymore, but he does continue to prospect. Prospecting can use a variety of media and touch points, one of which is phone conversation. If Frank wants to continue to prospect with one arm tied behind his back, he's lost an advantage.

Our system engages all of the prospecting tools that are available. My suggestion is that if we can recognize the flaws of cold calling, we can develop a system that doesn't take advantage of people or right-out lie to them. Instead, it recognizes and leverages the interest of the prospect first. More about that later.

Next we have "Unlock the Game: Cold Calling Doesn't Have to be Painful."[2] This Web site promotes pretty-boy Ari Galper. His shtick features "sincerity in sales" and a "deep understanding of human communication" due to his Master's Degree in instructional design. The most prominent concept on this Web site is Ari himself. I counted eighteen pictures of him, not to mention the various nonsensical video lectures. I think you should get a day job, Ari!

I found an article from an online property named All Business entitled "Tips for Successful Cold Calling."[3] This organization was so proud of its article on cold calling that the editors did not bother to cite an author. Wow! The article compiled the basic, general BS that most so-called experts highlight regarding this topic. You know the shtick: overcome your reluctance; research your prospects; prepare an opening statement; make gatekeepers your allies; stay focused; avoid common mistakes; stick with it. This sounds more like a high school basketball coach preparing teenagers for an upcoming tournament than instruction for a professional curriculum designed to equip sales professionals for vital prospecting activity.

> "There must be some way out of here," said the Joker to the Thief.
> "There's too much confusion. I can't get no relief."
>
> —Bob Dylan, 1968

Another cold-calling "coach" named Mark Sanford owns the URL www.coldcalling.com.[4] While I admire his ability to find a great Web site address, his material is nothing more than an outmoded Dale Carnegie pitch. Below are excerpts from his well-written, yet substance-lacking article entitled "Rules for Maximizing Call Effectiveness."

> "Here are some practical suggestions that will help you make the most of your calling efforts in the coming months. 1. Establish daily goals of how many calls you are going to make. If you have problems making as many calls as you want, begin counting pick-ups, not contacts. Begin with one or two a week if that is your present calling rate."

One or two cold calls per week? Come on, Mark! Get real!

> "See your cold calls as a game in which the objective is to "win" by getting the prospect to either agree to receive your marketing piece or to see you face-to-face."

Cold calling is NOT a game, Mark. And getting the prospect to agree to receive a piece of marketing is a colossal failure. In fact, that plays right into the hands of the prospect to get you off of the phone so he or she can get back to work. Wake up, man!

Maybe the two most incalculably deceptive books on the subject are *Selling to Vito* and *The Power to Get In*, written by Anthony Parinello and Michael Boylan respectively. These con artists purport the same underdeveloped cold-calling script, which goes something like this:

> **Sales Professional:** *Hi, Sally. This is Bob Johnson from XYZ Company. Is Mr. Williams in?*
> **Sally (Admin):** *No, he isn't. May I take a message?*
> **Sales Professional:** *Do you keep his calendar?*
> **Sally (Admin):** *Yes, I do. What is this regarding?*
> *(This sequence is where their systems break down entirely.)*
> **Sales Professional:** *I am looking to schedule a meeting with him to introduce him to our suite of X products and share with him how we saved COMPETITOR more than $1 million in operating costs over a twelve-month period.*

I recognize that the aforementioned pitch has a few good elements. But every sales rep on the planet uses the same basic chatter. Come on, Tony. Come on, Michael. Get real. You guys have created selling systems?

> Clowns to the left of me,
> Jokers to the right,
> Here I am, stuck in the middle with you.
>
> —Stealers Wheel, 1973

In reality, they are nothing more than hyperbole cleverly masked in simple language and remedial concepts. The more I research what is written and spoken by supposed authorities regarding the topic of cold calling, I am reminded of certain lyrics sung by Tom Petty and Stevie Nicks in 1981:

"Baby, you could never look me in the eye. Yeah, you buckle with the weight of the words. Stop draggin' my ... Stop draggin' my ... Stop draggin' my heart around."

There are a lot of so-called experts flying around the country and/or shouting loudly over the Web's reach regarding the topic of cold calling. To most of them, I want to say, "Stop dragging the hearts of sincere people around. Leave them alone and allow them find a real system that brings genuine guidance, structured accountability, and real substance to assist with a difficult, yet powerful topic."

The one thing that all of these "experts" have in common is that they all understand how to sell to salespeople. They know that people hate cold calling, so they suggest that you don't do it anymore. They know that you are untrained and afraid of contacting new accounts, so they claim to have the secret to success. But despite the fact that they claim to be professional salespeople, the only people they are selling are other salespeople. *The Must-React System* has a proven history of reaching senior-level executives through cold calling. But it can be applied to any type of prospecting.

Another problem with cold calling is that many salespeople have *lost the discipline of cultivating an authoritative tone.* A big percentage of selling and prospecting over the phone has to do with tone. What I mean by that is the strength and knowledge that is conveyed through both your word choice and also the inflection of the voice. Imagine a sleazy car salesman. Or better yet, please recall Jack Lemmon's character from *Glengarry Glen Ross.* There is a sales tone to his voice. Despite what the person says, you really believe he or she is trying to rip you off! It's helpful to analyze your voice while you are talking to prospects. What is the tone *conveying?* What are you saying by the *way* you are saying it? We'll talk more about this later. For now, it is important to understand that you can call with a tone of defeat. It lets your prospect know that you don't even believe they are going to meet with you. I can guarantee you will not gain entry to new customers if you have a tone of defeat.

Cold calling isn't the only problem. Let's remember that the problem is prospecting. Cold calling is just one part of the larger whole. E-mail contact is another area of prospecting that is poorly planned and executed. Marketing departments send rich product-centric e-mail blasts to customer lists built on title and type of company. Despite the tragically low response rate (less than a fraction of a percent), most companies continue to increase their e-mail marketing budget.[5]

Why? Because e-mail is a low-cost delivery vehicle. It is easy to produce. It is easy to deliver. And even if only .05% responds to the e-mail, it is still considered a success. This is mind-boggling. When you look at the e-mail marketing "gurus," you find a bunch of information about best days and times to send, best IP addresses to send from, etc. I feel like I'm the only sane person in the room when I talk to people about their e-mail strategy. Why do people keep sending out the same tired marketing e-mails with bright colors and pictures and about ten pages of text? Wake up! No one reads it!

I'm not just concerned about the marketing e-mails that are sent out en masse. Let's consider the typical sales introductory e-mail.

Mr. Williams,

Per my prior dialogue with Jan today, I would like to introduce you to ABC Software and our enterprise-wide software solutions.

Further, I would like to share with you the benefits yielded at competitor X. Are you available to meet with me the week commencing September 15?

If you are not available at that time, please offer an alternative. Thank you so much!

Sincerely,

Jenna Johnson, ASM Chicago
312 555 4048 (office)
312 555 1264 (cell)

Normally, these types of messages will include several marketing PDF documents attached. This e-mail has nothing that appeals to an executive's concerns or interests. It is entirely dependent upon the name of the product and the slight possibility that this prospect might care what you've done at other companies. It has no sense of urgency, so it fails to convince the reader that he or she has been contacted for any specific reason. Instead, it convinces him or her that it is merely individualized spam. And what about those attachments? You have only killed the one opportunity for a response to this e-mail, which is "please provide more information." This response is normally just to allow him to say he reviewed your documentation and is not interested at this time. But since you included the documents, you now have no chance of communication. There is nothing additional you can provide to him, so there is no reason for him to engage in dialogue.

Not only are people poorly trained; there is a trend in companies across the globe to shorten their vendor lists. Companies don't want to evaluate new vendors. It's a fact. There *is* a secret list of approved vendors. How many times have you contacted a prospect and they have told you they only do business with preferred vendors? How about this one? They tell you they have already issued a request for proposal (RFP) for your product. How is it possible that you have missed this opportunity? Your company is normally involved in these evaluations; you are recognized in your field as a leader; and yet, you are not privy to this opportunity. Unless you are in a very unique market, it is very likely that the companies you are trying to get into already have vendors that offer a similar solution to yours. Depending on how large they are, they probably have several vendors offering the same services. Corporate initiatives are geared toward getting a shorter list of "preferred" vendors, not a longer one! If a company wanted to talk to you, they would have already. The very fact that you are not invited to the dance will keep you from succeeding, unless you can get around their defenses.

There is a protective tendency companies have to deflecting new sales calls. They are desperate to avoid them. They are already crawling with more salespeople than they can handle. They create special offices to create special processes to deflect salespeople. Most companies have a "vendor box" where they will transfer sales calls and e-mails. I don't know whether anyone ever truly checks those messages, but I haven't gotten any responses. These are all ways that companies design themselves to keep salespeople out. It's no wonder that when you call a new account they are in such a big hurry to tell you they have no interest in talking to you.

On top of the fact that salespeople aren't trained at prospecting and companies don't want to add new vendors, it's difficult to reach anybody directly when you do try to contact them. Think about it this way: You don't like prospecting, so you do not develop a technique or strategy for doing it. Corporate deflection strategies are geared toward boxing you out. And even when you do connect to somebody, she simply feels insulted that you barged in without an invitation. Despite the abundance of contact lists and databases, it is hard to determine who your contact should be in any particular account. And many times, those lists and services are outdated. How many times have you called a company, only to be told your so-called contact hasn't worked there for years! Often, you get stuck communicating with an administrative assistant or someone who works in the same office, but you can never seem to reach the contact. A day of prospecting will sometimes yield only hundreds of unreturned voice mails and e-mails. Consider that once the contact hears your voice mail, if they even listen to it, they are asked not to talk to new vendors. Not to mention, there are hundreds of voice mails pouring in from other vendors as well. How overwhelming! No wonder you never receive a call back.

> The more I see, the less I know,
> The more I like to let it go.
>
> —Red Hot Chili Peppers, 2006

To make matters worse, you don't know what you don't know. You don't know if your prospects are interested in your product. And if they are, you don't know who's in charge of making that decision. If you do reach someone at a target company, he might not even be involved with your project. Or worse, he's in bed with your competition! It could take months, even years, to learn the political landscape of a company. And by that time, your competition has been alerted to your presence and has created a smear campaign against you. You need a way to get your bearings in an organization quickly. But first things first: you need to find an inside champion, a coach, someone who will guide you through the account. But how do you find that person, and why should he or she help you when you do?

Another difficulty you face when prospecting is that there is a world of difference between the communication styles of talking on the phone, writing an e-mail, and speaking face-to-face. And, most likely, each company you have to deal with will react differently to each of those approaches. But there is a special culture of prospecting. There are administrative assistants that are trained to deflect sales calls; there are gatekeepers who will stall your entrance or sabotage you; and there are the sneaky internal competitors who might pretend that they are interested in your product long enough to keep you away from the real buyer while they close a sale. With these types of adversities, failure and defeat are the only things you take from prospecting.

If you aren't hung up by any of these obstacles, consider this one: people have a tendency not to trust someone they don't know. I tend to believe this is because they are barraged both at home and at work with cold calls and spam soliciting everything from credit card insurance to prescription drugs. The very environment of prospecting is tainted by the perception that it is all a scam. Try to imagine the feeling your prospects have when you launch into the old sales pitch of how much money your company has saved such and such a client. They are thinking about how this is like all the other calls that they have received. Even if your company is offering a legitimate product that is well-recognized, you are in a position that people do not trust. Developing a better story or anecdote is only going to make you sound slightly different from everyone else. Prospecting needs a total overhaul to be effective.

The net-net is that prospecting doesn't make many of you feel successful. You would rather put your time into developing relationships with people who already talk to you at companies you already know. But there is plenty of money to be made with net-new customers. Simple economics says that if you aren't making money from the customers, then your competitor is. So prospecting is a must for any company that hopes to succeed in the long-term. You might feel like you're faced with a catch-22. Don't worry. We have an answer for the prospecting conundrum.

What's the Answer?

I personally started a direct-response sales company specializing in selling a variety of technology products that grew from three employees to fifty employees in approximately three years. Annual revenue grew to $20 million during that same time frame. Ultimately, my board of directors and I sold the company to our largest, most strategic marketing partner for a valuation of $30 million. It was a great run! I recall being interviewed by a local journalist, who was writing an article highlighting the company's staggering growth. When I shared with her why we experienced such growth, she continued to harangue me with the same question, "What was the unique product that you were able to sell into a hot market at exactly the right time? Where did you get all of your product knowledge and market insight?"

At that time, I simply could not articulate it to a total stranger, but our success had little to do with any single product. Our entire success could be attributed to a profound introductory messaging system named *The Must-React System.* It was, unquestionably, the key to my company's amazing growth and subsequent success. Through *Must-React,* my sales team could secure meetings with senior executives, almost on-demand! By properly executing *Must-React,* we created an enormous pipeline of prospects that translated into revenue regularly and consistently. There was no magic bullet of market expertise or industry knowledge that I had and my competitors didn't. It was entirely based on our ability to develop new relationships at executive levels that turned into big business.

There is a reason that I have been able to set these types of meetings and to train others to do so. Throughout this book, I am going to share stories about how I have held meetings with C-level executives at a majority of the Fortune 500 companies, how I secured private appointments with a prime minister, a rock star, and many more. All of these have been possible because I have "cracked the code" on prospecting.

> You may write me down in history with
> your twisted, bitter lies,
> You may trod me down in the very dirt,
> And still like the dust I'll rise
>
> —Maya Angelou, 1978
> —Benjamin Chase Harper, 1995

The culture of phone sales can be understood and manipulated through several rules that I have developed; the old adage about working smarter, not harder, is true. Prospecting is a unique practice that needs to be developed and honed. Some of the methods and practices we prescribe may seem counterintuitive. But that's only because you have been used to thinking about prospecting as step 1 of many steps in your sales cycle. While that may be the case from the perspective of your sales organization, if you communicate that to the customer, you will never receive entry. What needs to be communicated to your prospects clearly and consistently is that this is not a part of your sales process. When you sit down to prospect, you need to convince yourself that that you are not a salesperson. In fact, if you execute the principles of *The Must-React System* properly, you are not inviting your prospects to attend a sales call. No, not at all. You are inviting them to attend a research-based briefing that contains compelling information that is educational and relevant to your target buyer. You and your team are perceived as research experts who are "briefing" select prospects on the results of your recently completed research project. You are now a source of counsel and direction. If you can convince yourself of these things, your customers will hear it in your voice. Through this change of presentation, you will be able to build an environment of trust between you and the customer. If you have truly found a pain-point for their organization, the transition between trusted advisor and sales executive will be natural and welcomed.

When I tell people this at training sessions, they sometimes feel like this is bait-and-switch maneuver, where you offer one thing and deliver another. This is not what is happening. I do not advise scheduling a meeting with your prospect to provide counsel and guidance, only to show them the old tired presentation of your product. *That* is a failure to deliver. What I am advising is to actually provide a level of information that is germane and pertinent to your client that points them in the direction of your solution set but never actually explicitly mentions your products. If this type of presentation gets your customer to react and begin asking more questions, you know you've developed that trust, and you can begin to offer the suggestions and expertise that your products and solutions provide. We will develop an entire presentation of this process throughout the book. The point here is that some of these elements may seem like they will not accomplish your goals. Through our research and anecdotes, we will show how they have worked for others. And, hopefully, you will try them out for yourself.

You might be thinking to yourself, "For whom is this book written?" Is it an introductory text, or have I geared it toward seasoned professionals? Is it just for inside sales and marketing groups that work exclusively over the phone? From my experience, I have found that *Must-React* is equally effective regardless of level of experience or role in the organization. *The Must-React System* can work for a brand-new inside sales rep or a vice president of sales with twenty-plus years of experience. I will tell you about the success of several inside teams I have trained. Some of my most successful pupils had no prior sales training at all! The consistent element in all my successful students is that they were willing to put away some of their initial reservations and give it a try. Many of my students have taken the elements that I present and used them to gain entry into the next step in their personal career development. It is important, however, that I state that this book targets professionals who work with high-ticket, complex products that require long sales cycles. My next book will address applying *Must-React* to transactional sales with shorter sales cycles.

After discussing the principles of *The Must-React System*, we will talk about how to implement them in your calling, e-mailing, and presentations going forward. The elements of *Must-React* are guides. You may not use all of them simultaneously. You might use some with one customer and then switch on your next call. But learning how to blend and use *Must-React* can take time. I suggest using the basic outlines that I provide as your starting point. They are proven to be effective, and they will yield the quickest results for you.

CHAPTER 1

Bad Habits Exposed

Several years ago, I was asked to set up an inside-sales team. Some of the members of the team had already been hired, and I was going to fill out the rest with new hires. Our job requirements stated that we wanted all of the applicants to have five or more years of relevant experience. After the hiring process was completed, I began my training: we set up specific industry solutions, built presentations, and the team was rocking.

Well, almost rocking. There was one member who had come from a financial services background and wasn't quite "getting it." He sat through the same training as the rest of the group, but for one reason or another, he wasn't employing the techniques. The leaders in the group were exceeding their goals and quotas quickly, but John was having trouble meeting the minimum expectations. He didn't seem to understand the elements of *Must-React*. He would deliver old sales lines that he had used in the past and not the new script I had written. He had a tone of voice that screamed "sales!"

I was concerned about John's longevity in the company if he continued to lag behind the others. I also wondered if I had missed something during my training. Perhaps he hadn't understood the methodology. I took my normal course of action to correct the problem. I spent hours in what I call "clinic time," or one-on-one training. We made calls together, and I offered critique about specific areas of improvement. Every time we met, he seemed to recognize the areas I was critiquing. He even agreed that they were areas of weakness that he would develop. But after several months, he had not changed at all! I was at my wits' end. Finally I realized that even though he understood the basic elements of *Must-React*, he didn't *trust* them. He had developed a safety blanket in his old techniques. For reasons I couldn't understand, he wasn't able to let go of the old and grab onto the new. I had never met someone who was so entrenched in old sales habits. Needless to say, I had to initiate a separation with this particular employee.

As CEO of a consulting firm that specializes in sales practices, I have had the opportunity to evaluate literally thousands of sales representatives in industries ranging from healthcare to financial services and insurance to manufacturing. And, for the most part, regardless of the product or solution being distributed or the market that is targeted, one fact remains the same: salespeople are salespeople. Some are stronger than others, but everyone needs improvement. Let me give you a few examples.

Bad Habit #1: Fear of the Phone

Despite being some of the most seemingly confident and attractive personalities, most salespeople are afraid of that big black thing on their desk. I'm not talking about the computer. Most salespeople are afraid of the phone. They are afraid of getting on it and calling their customers. I remember years ago, I was training a group of young people on how to use *Must-React*. After basic training in the priciples of *Must-React*, I felt they would be able to learn from spending a day with the top rep in their field. We invited a guy in from the East Coast to share about his success and show us how he presented the company on his calls. When we scheduled the meeting, he was full of enthusiasm. He thought it was a great idea. And he had some new ideas he was going to let us in on!

This rep was supposed to be a "bright shining star" in the company. So we all expected great things. But, as we progressed through our day, there wasn't a lot of work being done on the phone. I kept suggesting that we stop talking about calling customers and actually call somebody. That was the reason he had been invited in the first place. But each time, he deflected my suggestion with an excuse. We spent an entire day together and never heard him make a single call. He was just plain scared of the phone.

This is a normal experience for young salespeople. If you aren't used to the ups and downs of prospecting, there is a learning curve. As good salespeople mature, they grow out of that fear. It is necessary for the success of the rep and the success of the company.

Bad Habit #2: Less About You, More About Me

Most salespeople love to talk about themselves or their company. This has usually been assumed to be a good thing. Sales managers often tell their reps to learn a few stories about the company's victories and then tell them to everyone they meet. The bad habit that this creates is that we "smell" like a sales rat when we do that. Every salesperson is telling her clients how much she has saved such and such a client. It might be a great story, but the focus is on showing how great your company is. Several years ago, I was performing a sales audit for a division of 3M. (A sales audit is an in-depth analysis of a company's sales procedure and ability.) One of the sales reps I spoke with exemplified this habit.

The rep was Cliff Hanks. I was calling each of the salespeople under the pretense of being a consultant who had been retained by a large corporation that was actively retiring an old operating system and installing a new one, which meant that we were going to be purchasing new enterprise-wide applications. Cliff was completely abrasive as I began to ask him some basic questions about his company and products. He insisted that I introduce him to the company I was representing. He told me that he didn't deal with consultants.

After I assured him that my client was only going to be extending an invitation to the vendors I advised, Cliff began diving into a long history of his company and some of its recent wins. He wouldn't let me get a word in edgewise. His knowledge of the company was impressive, but it was as if he forgot about my initiative. I couldn't have told him about our budget, timeframe, political map, final decision-maker information, or requisite activities to close if I wanted to. To top things off, Cliff told me that his company was usually the third company considered for these types of projects! A smarter rep would have said that his company was a leader in this space and always a member of the short list. Cliff hadn't even taken the time to ask me if we had considered any of these other vendors. After a few minutes, he seemed to recognize his mistake and told me that they had won their last five deals.

After an extensive discussion about their wins and the value-add they had given to customers, we ended the call with *no next step*! Cliff was so focused on his own company and telling me about their victories and success, he never gained an understanding of my project and didn't schedule a next-step meeting. This is a classic sales bad habit. If I were a real consultant, I would have smelled this sales technique a mile away. I would have never advised my client to schedule time with him. And if I ever received a cold call with this approach, I would certainly decline.

Bad Habit #3: Selling in the Product Zone

If salespeople aren't talking about themselves or their company, they are talking about how great their product is. They love industry jargon. If they could take a step back for a moment, they would realize that people don't actually talk that way in the "real" world. Or if they do understand that type of language, they don't use it themselves. No matter how great your company or products are, the customers want to know that you know their needs and that you understand their business problems. I have done hundreds of evaluations of cold calls, and you can sense when the prospect "checks out;" nearly every time, it is right when the salesperson gets to the part of his pitch where he says "our product." Agh! We'll talk about the importance of staying in the "no-product zone" later. For now, it is important to understand that once you bring up a product on a cold call, you have decreased your chances of getting a next step by 83%.[6] If you are talking to an admin, you have almost completely destroyed your chance for success. They are told not to allow salespeople to schedule meetings. If they hear you mention the word "product," there is no way they are going to schedule a next step on behalf of their executive.

Bad Habit #4: Fear of Executives

I've had the opportunity to meet with heads of Fortune 500 companies across the United States. I always ask them how they like to be approached by a new vendor. They usually have four or five tips, but they all agree that salespeople need to assume a level of leadership and expertise when they are speaking with and presenting to executives. People in power want to be with other powerful people. They want to receive presentations that are delivered with conviction. And they want to be given direction and leadership throughout the sales cycle.

But salespeople are afraid of contacting executives. The reason is that they haven't received training on how to interact with executives and decision makers in companies. They are comfortable with their peers, but they feel like they are in a different world when they enter the office of an executive.

When I was twenty-six years old, I got a job at a very successful software company. As usual, I was out of my element. I had pushed my way through the interview process, beating others with ten or fifteen years of sales experience. I was young, but using the same tenacity that had granted a meeting with Jesse Jackson in college, I was able to convince the vice president of sales I was qualified. I was given a territory in the Midwest and paired up with one of the company veterans for some initial training.

I sat in his cube for several hours, listening to him go on and on about how much he knows about the product and the industry. He had been around for a long time. I have to admit his knowledge of the industry was impressive, but I didn't understand how it would appeal to an executive. Most people would have assumed that he knew what he was talking about and just continued to listen. But I interrupted.

"Can you tell me one concept or idea that actually appeals to the executives at your companies?" I asked.

He turned bright red.

"Alright, hotshot," he barked, "you get a meeting!"

Nothing I had ever done should have made me assume that I would be able to get a meeting with an executive. This was a David and Goliath situation. But I had smaller victories, like being on the "Super Q" in St. Louis and meeting with Jesse Jackson. How much harder could this be? I made a couple dials that just went to voice mail. But after my challenge, I had to prove to this guy what I was capable of accomplishing on the phone.

The third call was to the CFO of the largest insurance company in his territory. I attacked the call aggressively. He tried to tell me that he was unable to meet with our company that week because he was traveling. I deflected his objections by telling him that I understood he had a busy schedule that week, but I doubted it would clear up in the near future. We needed to meet with him by the end of the week. I told him we would call him between meetings and closed for a time later that week. He finally agreed, and we met later that week.

By the end of my first year, I was the top sales rep in the company. Others had more product knowledge or industry experience. But because of my ability to overcome the fear of contacting executives, I was able to build larger pipelines faster than my peers. This was a skill that I continued to develop through my career, and today, it is part of my principle of "people need leadership." There is no room for fear and doubt when contacting executives. They demand leadership. You need to provide it.

Bad Habit #5: Buying into the Hype

We work in an industry driven by hype. I have been in what feels like hundreds of meetings where the manager gave a rousing speech that sent all of the employees back to their desks ready to sell—sell—sell! But the feeling died before the end of the day because there was no substance behind the hype.

There was one sales manager who typified this experience for me. We'll call him Mike Phillips. Mike was a "life of the party" kind of guy. He was as colorful a manager as you could imagine. The first time I sat in one of his sales meetings, I was shocked. The first reason was that he was a very powerful speaker. His whole team responded to his stories, jokes, and even reprimands. He spoke with conviction and power. But the second reason I was shocked was that Mike was able to speak for nearly an hour and say almost nothing! It was all hype. You could write the script. "Make the coffee. Turn out the lights. Dress for success. Sell something. Stay active. Hope is not a strategy." Blah! I felt like I had sat through the same tired pep talk since my first sales job.

The tragedy of these meetings is that they reinforce old and ineffective sales methodologies. They boost your spirits for a moment, but after the feeling fades, they have longer-lasting effect. They teach you that in order to be successful, you just need to do more of what you are currently doing. This assumes that people intuitively know how to cold call, prospect, develop sales, and close deals. But as we discussed in the introduction, this isn't true. People aren't well trained. So doing more of the same is a recipe for disaster.

If you get a group of salespeople who are addicted to selling with bad habits and you tell them to work harder, they aren't going to magically overcome all of their previous practices. They might do more work, but more of the same is only going to result in continued failure. But people buy into the hype because it removes responsibility. If Mike told his guys to send out ten e-mails a day, they would do it. But they were the same ineffective e-mails that had never worked in the past. So nothing was accomplished, but the salespeople felt safe because they had accomplished an objective. People buy into the hype because they are afraid to face their inadequacies and seek professional training.

If you are a sports fan, you'll remember Tom Landry, coach of the Dallas Cowboys from 1960 to 1988. Tom was a great football coach who revolutionized the game with many of his defensive and offensive innovations. One of his greatest contributions as a coach was in the pep talk he gave his team during halftime. But Landry's pep talks weren't merely motivational; they were instructional. He pointed out specific technique adjustment for specific players.

Most coaches were like the sales managers we've been talking about, full of passion and fire. They would yell and scream "Hit harder! Run faster! Jump higher!" This might have energized the team, but it gave them no practical advice to apply to their sportsmanship. They just tried doing the same things with more heart.

Landry coached differently. If he wanted a certain player to change, he would give him specific advice. He explained how to anticipate the moves of the other team by watching for cues and then gave instruction on how to react. His team did go on to hit harder, run faster, and jump higher. But they did so with practical information that they could apply every time they went on the field. Landry's Cowboys didn't just play harder. They matured and developed. At the end of his career, Landry had proved the merits of his style with two Super Bowl titles, five NFC titles, thirteen divisional titles, and a 270-178-6 record, the third most wins of all time for an NFL coach. A good sales manager needs to provide his team members with that type of information and training. If he does, he will be a champion like Landry.

There are hundreds of other bad habits which salespeople possess. These are only the major ones that will stand in the way of total success using The System. I advise you perform a self-evaluation or ask a peer to evaluate your calling.[1] You may feel uncomfortable letting another person listen to your calls and give you critique. But this is the best way to recognize fatal flaws and improve upon them.

Bad habits aren't developed without reason. They give comfort and support to us. We keep doing them out of practice. But even after we have stopped doing them, we feel drawn back in! This is simply because we have developed a comfortable way of selling through these habits. Even though the habit is getting

---

1   I have included a Self Evaluation form at the end of this book. I suggest that you complete it now. Then, after you have practiced some of the elements of *Must-React*, go back and reevaluate yourself. This is a good way to track your growth as you learn my principles.

in the way of your success, you will not want to destroy it because of the comfort it provides.

Despite the fact that these bad habits yield the same results time after time, people continue to use them. Consider the following: In an average week, typical executives spend 66% of their time out of the office, 35% of their time with customers, attend thirty-seven meetings, receive 360 pieces of mail, and receive 240 phone calls, 143 voice mail messages, and 288 e-mail messages.[7] You don't need to be a math wiz to figure out those decision makers at the companies you want to talk with are inundated by your peers and competitors. There is no good way for them to decide to hear some product pitches and not others. They don't care how much money you've saved their competition. They are overwhelmed by their responsibilities and the over-contact from salespeople like you. As soon as they hear your product pitch or smell the sales call, they eliminate it. They simple don't have time to deal with it. They have business concerns to resolve.

The fact that so many people are all using the same techniques and the same scripts to get into the same accounts creates a white noise for executives. They can't pay attention to all of the different details between you and your competition. You all sound the same. And they already have someone who can do that. Classic sales methodologies have taught students to distinguish themselves from their competition. Come up with a different perk or exciting story for your customer. If you can show them how you are different from the rest, they will be interested in talking to you. Unfortunately, this type of differentiation doesn't work, because no one is paying attention to the detail. They are listening for the first sign of a sales pitch. As soon as you've identified yourself as a salesperson, you can be eliminated. The answer is not *distinguishing* yourself from your competition. It's *removing* yourself from the competition. You need to stop thinking of yourself as a salesperson representing a company and a product. This is the model that has failed hundreds of salespeople already. It would be insanity to continue using it when you know it is going to fail! Prospecting cannot be a part of the sales process. In fact, *remove yourself from the sales process*! If salespeople are a nuisance, stop being a salesperson. You need to learn how to reinvent yourself so that instead of "smelling" like a sales rat or like a product-hack, you smell like information. You smell like assistance. You smell like research. You smell like big-brain data compilation.

> "The answer is not distinguishing
> yourself from the competition;
> it's removing yourself from the competition."

—Kraig Kleeman, 2002

This approach will radically change your style and your success rate. *The Must-React System* is designed to completely remove you from traditional selling. It insists that you enter the "no product zone," and it trains you to "brief" your prospects on research results that are highly relevant to them. Further, the briefings are cleverly designed to allow you to deeply qualify your prospects for possible sales opportunities.

But in order for this to work, you have to be ready to change. You have to realize that your way of doing things hasn't worked. You need to let go of your bad habits and devote yourself to practicing the elements of *Must-React* that I have developed. I'm not going to present another pep talk that leaves you high on emotional hype but clueless on how to succeed. I'm going to present you with ideas and concepts that will totally change your whole process of selling. If you really want to make your prospecting efforts work on both a company-wide and a personal level, you need to be willing to change.

By following the practices laid out in this book, you will be able to develop a clear and concise strategy for prospecting. You will be able to build cold-calling scripts and e-mail messaging that actually works. You will be overwhelmed with activity.

Often when I begin consulting engagements with new companies, I advise that they establish a tightly monitored demand-creation program. The response is normally a few chuckles and "that's a problem we'll gladly deal with when we reach it." But time after time, they are scrambling to deal with the massive influx of activity. Unfortunately, many of those early leads go to waste due to poor stewardship. I'm certain you will find similar results, so part of our discussion will focus on issues of defining and maintaining a demand-creation management tool. This will help you analyze the lead-generation events that are most effective, the follow-up messaging and qualification methods, and the contribution of those events to pipeline.

It's time to make prospecting prosperous.

CHAPTER 2

The Must-React System

The Must-React System is a philosophy of demand creation. It is founded on the belief that demand creation is a critical portion of every company's business operations. As such, it creates a way of thinking about demand creation that produces, tracks, and analyzes meaningful activity. It can and should be applied to every cold call, e-mail, and introductory presentation given. But it also directs the larger prospecting strategy of the company. In short, these methods need to be learned by everyone from the Chief Sales and Marketing Officers to the entry level associates. In the following section, we will discuss the principles of *Must-React*. They are laid out in four chapters totaling eleven principles.

At the most basic level, *The Must-React System* attracts prospective buyers to attend an analyst briefing based on industry research. This briefing will allow you to qualify the prospect and build a vision for how your offerings can help them solve their needs.

Chapter 3 will discuss the necessary techniques to implement The System from the top down. Prospecting is not just about the feet on the street, the sales guys making the calls, or the presentations being given. It is also dependent upon a strong system for tracking and assessing the demand-creation process. We'll discuss how to make this work in your organization.

Chapter 4 will cover the first three principles of *Must-React*: Remove Yourself from the Sales Cycle, Core Value Declaration, and Create Appropriate Spaces. As we discussed previously, product-centric language is limited in its ability to appeal to executives. In order to gain attention with the decision makers in prospective accounts, you must learn to remove yourself from the sales cycle. This encompasses the way marketing mailings are written and mailed to the style and subject of introductory presentations. Every principle of *Must-React* is designed to remove you from the sales process.

Most industries possess demand-creation strategies that are ill-equipped to appeal to their targets on the basis of the target's true core values. This group tends to articulate either features or benefits, both of which are in error. *The Must-React System* is inherently designed to decode this type of language and translate it into senior executive core values through benefit-superset techniques.

Creating appropriate spaces teaches that people will feel more comfortable sharing certain aspects of their project and company goals in different environments. Instead of fighting this, we talk about how you can incorporate this into your strategy to deeply qualify every opportunity.

Chapter 5 introduces the principles of Enter the No-Product Zone and Less is More. Most companies incorporate product-centric dialogue within their introductory messaging. This type of messaging fails for a variety of reasons. The target typically gets dozens of product-centric calls daily and is immune to such calls that are centered on introducing him or her to a company and its products and services. The target has trained his or her staff to reject such meeting offers. Product-centric messages do not address the target's core values in any way. Entering the no-product zone is a way of creating a deliberate value of avoiding the product in question during all demand-creation events.

The principle of Less is More forces you to be frugal with your language. People are overwhelmed by information. From morning to evening, we are inundated by information from national, international, professional, and personal sources. Less is More simply states that you can communicate more if you communicate less. Corporations attempting to introduce themselves present entirely too much information. One analyst described current messaging practices as "incoherent, irrelevant, and non-germane to the target's core values."

Chapter 6 teaches the principles of Power Responds to Power and Peer Reacts to Peer. It is surprising that companies have not adapted these concepts more broadly. Power Responds to Power states that people of power will be more inclined to meet with your company if they are invited to do so by another person of power. Similarly, Peer Reacts to Peer teaches to appeal to the similarities between yourself and the clients that you are contacting.

Chapter 7 presents a group of closely interrelated concepts: People Require Leadership, Use Commanding Statements, Deadlines Really Work, and Offer Alternative Close Dates. Research indicates that tone represents 80% of what is communicated, towering over the power of persuasive words. Tone is not just something that is present in vocal communication. There is a tone to the way a sales campaign is run, the way a presentation is laid out and delivered, and even the way a company Web site is constructed. There is an abundance of passivity in current practices. People Require Leadership and Use Commanding Statements teach you how to develop messaging that will demand meaningful activity with authority.

Deadlines Really Work is a simple concept that is entirely overlooked. The simple incorporation of Alternative Close Dates into prospecting activities can transform the success rate of every company.

The elements of *The Must-React System* are essential for prospecting in the modern sales environment. Once these guiding principles are in place, our analytic tools can be applied to the demand-creation process to ensure proper execution on every prospecting campaign.

CHAPTER 3

The System Behind the System

In the introduction of this book, we discussed the errors in dialogue around prospecting. Many "pundits" have espoused wrong theories and have not just had an effect on the activity of prospecting. They have caused immeasurable damage to the entire sales process and the methodology for managing the sales process.

Methodologies like "VITO" (Very Important Top Officer) have led companies to adopt wrong data into their sales tracking and metrics. One company I worked for had a twenty-nine-step sales process. Twenty-nine steps! These steps included some reasonable activities, but mostly it was events such as "mail VITO letter." In practice, the field sales reps never followed these steps, and sales management never enforced them, but the CEO would blame reps for a failed deal if they had neglected to mail the VITO letter!

In reality, the sales force was only using a handful of the twenty-nine sales steps. But because the reporting system was so burdensome, and since it was being avoided anyway, it was not giving accurate or pertinent information to sales management or the board of directors.

This particular system was also designed to heavily track the sales process, but it had no capability to show the relationship between marketing efforts and sales production. This caused two problems. The first was that the demand-creation process was not being accurately tracked and managed. The second was that the marketing department was not being accurately tied to its rightful contribution to revenue production. In a company that already marginalized the use of marketing, the marketing department was seen as increasingly useless because it appeared to have no bearing on revenue.

These issues are obviously interrelated. If marketing campaigns produced leads, there was no system in place to know how many of them had been contacted by the sales force. Questions like "How many had meaningful dialogue?" or even "How many had no interest?" could not be answered. This made it extremely difficult for the marketing group to determine which of their efforts were having the greatest outcome. All they could track was the number of names and numbers collected. But this was not an accurate way of tracking a successful marketing strategy. It was missing any tie to revenue.

So, with my guidance, the chief marketing officer fought for control of a portion of the inside sales group his company had. We used this group to provide the initial qualification data on the raw leads that were being produced from Web seminars, trade shows, marketing lists, etc. Based on tightly scripted qualification standards, that team was able to determine if an opportunity existed. They then obtained buy-in from sales management, and the opportunity was turned over to a field sales representative. This "hand off" provided a way for the CMO to tie his groups' efforts directly to revenue. It also gave him the power to use the sales tracking system to provide accountability for those leads. By simply using reports from the CRM database, we were able to determine which salespersons were following up on their leads and which were not. We were able to provide hard evidence to sales management that marketing was providing solid revenue opportunities but that lazy salespersons were botching them.

As time went on, we were able to provide information about how much annual revenue should be attributed to a specific trade show or cold-calling list. We were also able to show that the marketing efforts were driving customer interest and developing projects. This information was priceless for the CMO. Without it, he had no defense for his teams' projects besides total number of raw leads. They were into mass production because it was the only measure of success. But by applying a team of inside marketing people to qualify the raw leads and turn them into solid opportunities, he was able to justify his existence with dollar signs. When he went into quarterly meetings with our demand-creation metrics, he was able to provide information on the performance of each sales team, lead highlights in high-profile accounts, campaign effectiveness, and summaries of lead stewardship and distribution.

These numbers could be developed because of the strict tracking mechanism we put in place. Once a lead was place in the CRM database, it was tagged by our team. If it was advanced to a sales cycle, it was labeled as a hand off and therefore a qualified sales opportunity.

The sales and marketing group had determined that there were two legitimate types of hand offs: A-Class and B-Class. An A-Class hand off identified a project that was funded and budgeted. An A-Class lead additionally identified the decision maker as well as an inside coach that acknowledged the need for our solution. In order to qualify as an A-Class Lead, the B-Class hand off was designed to build project interest in companies. It required an internal champion who recognized the need for our solution and was willing to continue discussions with our sales team.

After a lead had been tagged as an A-or B-Class hand off, the marketing group was able to track when the account rep updated the lead. We tested two areas: how many days since the last update, and how many days since it was progressed to a new step in the sales cycle? These metrics allowed us to tell if the rep was actively engaging the lead by tracking the number of updates. But it was also able to tell us about the quality of attention being paid to the lead. A sales rep could be entering a note of "LVM" (left voice mail) every day but never progressing the lead in the sales cycle.

We also tracked the total number of hand offs that had actively contributed to the sales pipeline by tracking the dollar amounts associated with each lead. Once again, this allowed us to determine the quality of attention being paid to each lead. If lead hand offs weren't progressing into true projects with potential revenue value for the company, we wanted to determine if our marketing team was pushing leads to the sales team prematurely or if the sales team was neglecting to aggressively pursue the opportunities.

We tracked these metrics down to the sales group and even the individual salesperson. This allowed sales management to see which groups were updating the leads and which were letting them die on the vine. It also allowed sales management to see which reps were receiving the most leads. If management needed to, they could adjust their allocation of leads based on the lead stewardship of individual reps.

All of this was possible because of the intense scrutiny we applied through our tracking mechanism. And none of this would have been possible without a prospecting team that was qualifying the raw marketing leads and handing them off to field sales.

Marketing departments throughout the country will need to develop this type of system to continue justifying their existence. There is a diminishing amount of patience for departments of companies that are unable to tie themselves to revenue-producing activities. The most concrete way to determine marketing involvement in revenue is to deploy a prospecting team using *The Must-React System* to qualify sales opportunities and then to deliver them to the field. At that point, strict reporting guidelines can be measured and enforced.

CHAPTER 4

Give the People What They Want

A few years back, I was vacationing in Europe. At the same time, my brother was in Europe for several business meetings. We discussed our itineraries and figured out that we could probably meet in Greece for a classic guys' "yuck it up, hit the beach, and eat well" weekend. At the last minute, Karry's plans changed. He had no choice but to be at a large bank in Amsterdam at 8:00 am the following Monday morning.

Sadly, Greece was not going to work for him. We regrouped, and after some creative planning, we decided to simply move the location of the get-together to Amsterdam. With some reluctance, I caught a train from Brussels while Karry flew from the UK.

I arrived, exhausted from travel, and crashed in my hotel room. Karry showed up later that afternoon, and we decided to meet in the hotel bar for a few drinks before heading out for dinner. I was still pretty tired, but I was excited to catch up with my brother.

We got to the bar, which was full but not packed, and found a couple open stools. As we were having our drinks and catching up on recent happenings in each other's lives, we noticed a commotion toward the entrance of the bar. I looked over at the group entering the bar and recognized a familiar face. Bono. At first, I thought there was no way that it was actually Bono. I am a devoted U2 fan. The thought of actually being in the same bar as one of my heroes was extremely exciting. But it seemed too good to be true, so I chalked it up to a look-alike and went back to my discussion with Karry.

"You know, that guy looked just like Bono," I told him.

Karry looked over his shoulder at the group that had now made its way to a large circular booth in the corner.

"Dude," Karry responded, "that is unmistakably Bono!"

Over the next thirty minutes, we watched as several people would walk over to the table to try and speak with him. We laughed each time as the bodyguards explained that Bono was just trying to relax and enjoy himself. He wasn't in the mood for an impromptu fan club meeting. In all honesty, I think there were two groups of people in the bar: those who wanted to meet Bono and thought they might have a chance, and those who wanted to meet Bono but didn't want to look ridiculous getting pushed away from the table.

Karry started a debate about who would have the greater legacy, the Beatles or U2. We debated the point for a while and then switched to arguing over which U2 album was the best.

Painful as it was, people continued to approach the table over and over again without ever catching Bono's attention, only to be escorted away by a member of his entourage. I was laughing at the utter hopelessness of the attempts when Karry made a wager.

"Kraig, you claim in your sales training to be able to get a meeting with anybody on-demand, right?" he asked.

"Yes. It works every time."

"Right," he replied politely, but with some reserved skepticism.

"Well," he continued, "I bet you can't get a fifteen-minute meeting with Bono right now."

"Karry, don't be ridiculous. Where have you been for the last thirty minutes? Bono is not interested in meeting with anyone right now."

"I thought you said your system works every time. Are you saying it can't work now?" He was trying to get at me, and it was working.

"Alright," I said defensively, "what should we bet?"

"If you can get a meeting with Bono right now, I will pay for your hotel and all your expenses for the weekend. If you can't, you pay for mine."

This was the sort of reckless brotherly competition that had characterized our relationship since we were young boys. I knew from past experience that I had no choice in the matter. I either had to accept the challenge or concede failure. The expenses would no doubt be in the multiples of thousands of dollars for the weekend, but there was no way I was going to back down from this challenge.

I needed a strategy. I knew that unless I had something different than these other groupies, I was going to end up receiving the same patronizing look I had been giving to everyone else who failed. The first step of my methodology is to take yourself out of the sales process. You have to remove yourself from the normal noise that your target is always hearing.

The best way to do that is by tapping into the core value of your target. I began to ponder the obvious question: what is of importance to Bono? Being a longtime fan of U2 and having admired Bono's personal life, I queried myself regarding Bono's passions, life goals, etc. I decided that it would not be a good idea to approach him on the basis of his music, since he gets approached dozens of times daily on that topic. My mind harkened back to articles I have read in the past about his deliberate involvement in a variety of humanitarian efforts, which include fighting AIDS and other social issues that plague underdeveloped nations. I recalled that Bono has visited the White House, donated extraordinary amounts of money, and articulated his views on a number of TV news shows. He has shared audiences with Dick Cheney, Larry King, and numerous other "talking heads." He often described himself as a voice for the "poor of the earth."

After some thought, I decided that my only chance at getting a meeting with Bono was no different than getting a meeting with a senior executive at any corporation: I had to appeal to a topic that is absolutely core to his thinking! Bono is an amazing musician. He knows it and everyone tells him that. But what he cares about, what keeps him up at night, is his compassion for the poor and hurting throughout the world.

I geared myself up for one shot to grab his attention on an issue that mattered.

"Hey, Bono!" I shouted over to the bar.

His face looked my way.

"I am totally impressed by your personal support assisting developing nations that wrestle with difficult social issues like poverty, AIDS, food distribution, and under-education."

His ears now perked up!

"In fact," I continued, "I once was on the board of directors for an outreach to abandoned children in South America, and I understand how painfully difficult it is to get individuals from our modernized world to understand the plight of lesser developed nations!"

I lifted my drink and continued.

"And I just want to toast you for your steadfast commitment to be a voice for the poor of the earth!"

Bono lifted his bottle in a toast.

At first, that was it. Nothing happened right away, so I sat down and began to think about how Karry was going to spend the rest of the weekend rubbing my failure in my face. But then I noticed that Bono was talking to a member of his entourage. The man came over and told Karry and I that Bono would like to have a drink with us!

We ended up talking with him for more than thirty minutes about the wager, recent news, and a new campaign for AIDS prevention in Africa and China. We were able to discuss a variety of topics that would have never been possible had we not been invited to his table. This is called Creating Comfortable Space. (We'll talk later about how you can integrate it into your prospecting.) But never once did any of us speak a word about music. It was all about his interests in bringing genuine assistance to the "poor of the earth."

Why did Bono meet with me, even though many others had tried to meet with him in that moment? Why did he accept my request? Mostly because I did not approach him on the same basis that everyone else approaches him, which is as a fan of his music. Rather, I approached him on the basis of what is *absolutely core* to his personal values. People are much more inclined to discuss topics near and dear to their hearts than they are to discuss sterile, innocuously boring topics. And while Bono has an astonishing track record of creating amazing music mixed with powerful lyrics, that is not a topic where his heart is most tightly bound. His heart is bound-up in organizing humanitarian relief for people groups, nations, and the poor of the earth.

The number-one problem with most salespeople is that they are too self-centered. This isn't a moral critique; it's a professional one. Salespeople grab onto a great story or benefit of their product, and they insist on telling it to their customers and prospects. Even if the prospect is obviously not interested, many salespeople will continue to blunder their way through the same canned phrases and glory stories until the client leaves or hangs up. They don't take the time to understand how and why their client would be interested in this information.

As true as that is, the top decision makers in sales and marketing organizations are even worse. They are completely infatuated with their products' abilities and the customer list that they have. They have the feeling that just because they have been able to convince other large companies to purchase their solution, everyone else should just flock to them instinctively. They produce flashy, glossy, product-centric e-mail blasts and marketing collateral. So much of this effort is devoted to a "keeping up with the Joneses" mentality. If my competitor's product can go fast, mine can go faster. This type of prospecting is the equivalent of the rejected groupies in the bar with Bono. Buyers are *initially* less interested in what your product does than they are that you understand what is important to them.

The power of persuasion depends entirely on your sales organization's ability to understand what keeps your client up at night. This is what we mean when we talk about core values. Bono was a rock star, but his core value was the "poor of the earth." Since thousands of fans across the world have praised him for his music, it would be foolish for me to lump myself in with the thousands of other fans. Instead, by appealing to one of the deepest issues of Bono's concern, I became a fellow solider in his battle against world poverty. I wasn't one of thousands; I was someone who understood what *really* matters.

So, how do you remove yourself from the sales process and determine your prospect's core value? Simply put, give the people what they want. What do the executives want? This is a different question than what are they going to buy. Because they may want to avoid risk, or to retain customers, or to increase revenues, but they will buy something to deal with those concerns based on what they feel is the best strategy for accomplishing those goals. So banks and insurance companies don't buy client retention; they buy electronic statement delivery. But they don't want to talk to a sales rep about electronic statement delivery; they want to talk about strategies for customer retention. Once they can understand that their business problem is going to be mitigated by a certain strategy, then you can present the product information. The point is that there is no room for product-centric discussions in prospecting.

This is essentially different from the old solution-based selling theory. What we are concerned with is not presenting a solution to a problem. We are concerned with developing a rapport with a buyer based on his or her concerns. Once that rapport is established, you can employ a variety of different sales strategies for progressing and closing the deal.

Developing a Core-Value Declaration from scratch can be difficult, especially if you have never done it before. Normally when I present this concept, I will provide hands-on examples with my client's current sales presentations. In this book, we will have to depend on the power of narrative example.

To begin with, you need to develop an understanding of your prospect. This requires a certain level of industry knowledge. But you don't need to be an expert in every industry and on every job in a corporate hierarchy. I've worked with industry directors who had huge brains in their respective field but they didn't instinctively recognize how their knowledge could be used to lure in new prospects. Generally, if you are able to identify the top three concerns in the industry you sell in, you can use one of those. You don't need to be an expert in all of the issues.

You do need to have a basic understanding of the titles in an organization that are assigned the responsibility of dealing with those issues. The CEO of a company may be genuinely concerned about a problem, but what does his role in the organization require him to do? He needs to strategize and delegate and manage. If he tried to go to every meeting and attend every task-force lunch, he would be taxed beyond his limits. It is likely that there is a single person or a group of people in your prospective accounts that has been assigned the responsibility for helping the CEO sleep at night about the issue that you have identified. Having a meeting with the CEO can give you great amount of support, but you might realize that the issue you've identified will never directly affect him. Maybe your contact is actually the vice president of finance. Whoever your contact is, it is important to understand what his or her concerns are.

Let's discuss how I build a core value for a client. To begin with, I establish who we are looking for and where we are looking for him. Who are we looking for? Do you sell to the chief financial officer or the director of human resources? Maybe you sell to the vice president of operations or the call center manager. Although we aren't going to present our product initially, that doesn't mean that we don't shoot for the target buyer. This is the person we want to be talking to about product. We just know that we cannot go in with product guns blazing. We need to have a little more finesse and polish when we are building the relationship.

Some companies I have worked with have a clearly established target base. Not only have they been selling products, they have been paying attention to who the buyer is. Other companies are not as astute. They may have a very healthy sales rate, but perhaps they have not grown to the point where they have clearly defined their buyer. If this is the case, I recommend doing an analysis of the more successful sales cycles to identify a common buyer title. Alternatively, working with industry analysts can provide a clear target buyer.

Once you have established your target buyer's title, you may need to focus down to a specific industry market. If your company has products for healthcare and insurance companies you may need to build separate core-value messages for each of those markets. It is also important to note the size of the organization that is most likely to purchase your product. When we have established who we are looking for and where we are looking for them, we know who our audience is. Now we need to figure out what keeps them awake at night.

So, how do you put your message in terms that meet the core value of the prospect? At times, this is going to feel like putting a square peg in a round hole. But it is important to remember that when you are building a new relationship, you are not starting with the product; you are starting with needs and concerns. There are two ways you can think about this.

The first is: start from the product and think about what need it was made to fill. How has that need changed or developed since the product was first released? What is the "newsworthy" issue around that need today?

Early in my career, I made acquaintance with an exceptional young man. Our wives had become friends and, as the result, he and I came together for occasional parties and social events. To both his dismay and mine, the women of our lives had a significant falling-out that never resolved itself and, sadly, our personal friendship faded.

Just four years ago, I was in my office when my administrative assistant alerted me that Joe Tinnerello was on the telephone. I had not seen nor spoken with Joe in many years, though I had admired him from a distance during his tenure as senior vice president of sales and marketing at a large, publicly traded software company. I had greatly admired watching "Joe T" (as he was affectionately known) successfully grow his firm's sales from $3 million in annual sales to nearly $100 million.

His fingerprints were all over that company's glorious run, which included a lucrative IPO (initial public offering)! As markets matured and times had changed, Joe had a tall request. It was time for his firm to greatly expand its efforts at recruiting "net-new" prospects. Though we had not connected on a personal level in many years, he had heard about the powerful results of *The Must-React System* sales consulting that I had begun. He was inquiring as to whether it could be successfully applied to enterprise software sales.

In short order, my team and I deployed a unique version of The System that had profound results. Within thirty days, his sales teams were conducting briefings (our new term for sales calls) with chief information officers, chief legal officers, chief compliance officers, and chief financial officers, almost on-demand. On a monthly basis, they were scheduling more than fifty meetings per week with the company's prime C-Level targets. *The Must-React System* had completely transformed the company's selling model.

The key to our success in gaining these meetings was developing new core value around a twenty-year-old product. During that time, a lot had changed in the business world, but the essential "pitch" had never changed. Joe's sales force continued selling the same thing because nothing drastic had changed with the product. This hadn't been a problem in their current customer base. These customers understood the product, knew the company, and had their own strategies for how to use it. But when our team came in, they were stalling in the current customer base too. The customers had trouble seeing where this old product fit in their new business strategy.

We evaluated the reasons the product had been developed, its strengths when it started in the market, and the growth of the product through the past twenty years. Then we asked ourselves how this product was newsworthy today. We all knew it was a good product, but where did it fit in the business strategy of companies in world of e-commerce and Sarbanes-Oxley requirements? We discovered that although their product had always been used to reduce the amount of paper used in a company, they were no longer dealing with the larger business issues behind that decision. The sales managers were still promoting cost savings as the big business driver. And at a certain part of the sales cycle, they were right. But during the introduction period, we needed to express the *core value* of the people who were trying to lower paper use.

In the insurance practice, we realized that the product had a strong appeal to directors of sales who were eager to retain their sales agents. Research showed that insurance companies struggled to keep agents hired. Turnover was high in the sales force, and every sales manager was looking for ways to keep their team intact. We also identified that study had shown agents strongly desired up-to-date information on all of their clients' policy information. By synthesizing the data, we were able to develop a core value that spoke to the vice president of sales in insurance companies. The message was Optimizing Agent Performance and Retention. This was the answer to the concerned VP of sales. It was also undergirded by research showing how electronic access to documents was a top strategy for retention. We weren't pitching product and cost reduction anymore; we were pitching business strategy for the one thing that kept our prospect awake at night. Core value had replaced product.

Another way to determine the core value of your prospect is to start from the industry. What are the major issues or concerns for the industry as a whole? Is it legislation that is forcing a business change? Is it attracting and maintaining new customers? Whatever it is it will be plastered across the trade publications; it will be the topic of the industry trade shows; and it will be producing an overwhelming amount of data. This creates a perfect storm for your ability to use the Core-Value Declaration to secure a meeting. When a topic gains national or international attention, it is discussed beyond apprehension. Every consulting group tries to produce a definitive knowledge share for the business community. But because there is so much information going on, and because executives are so pressed for time, there is often a wealth of people who need an executive summary of the information. It would be impossible to produce a general report of all of the information on the market. Instead, you need to define the problem in terms of a strategy that integrates your product or service.

Whichever way you identify the *core value* of your customer, you aren't finished there. It is not simple enough to know that your customers are concerned about losing customers or employees. You need to be able to communicate that need to them in a concise phrase that is no more than one sentence long. This phrase should conjure up an image of the larger discussion and then address the specific strategy that you are presenting. This is going to be your *Core-Value Declaration*. It is not a paragraph-long explanation of a problem. It is a one-sentence description of the value using relevant industry language or buzzwords.

The core value should be the first thing out of your mouth when you are cold calling; it should be the most prominent feature of every introductory e-mail you send; it should be displayed on your booth at trade shows. *Core value* is what gets you invited to the dance. It's what makes Bono nod in your direction at the bar. This is the hook that appeals to your customer just enough that they need to respond. We aren't concerned with closing the sale at this point. We are trying to create dialogue. We need interaction. Any response is good response with net-new customers. Once you get a reaction, the odds of gaining an introductory meeting are increased by a factor of ten. Even if the reaction you receive is negative, you have created a conversation where you can begin to battle the prospect on their relationship to your topic. Out of this conversation, you will either be able to gain a meeting with them or you will be directed to the appropriate person in the organization.

Now imagine for a moment the reaction on Bono's face, once he had invited Karry and I over to his table at the bar, if we had assaulted him with requests for autographs and discussion of his music. As you can guess, he would have had us removed immediately. This is the same problem you face when meeting with new clients, and this leads us into the next principle of *The Must-React System*: Creating Safe Space. This principle is based on the fact that introductory meetings need to be conducted in a space that allows the prospect to open up and share meaningful information. The safe space that The System creates is a *Must-React* Briefing. This briefing is based on the topic of your Core Value. It includes a variety of industry information, several slides of suggested best practices, and suggestions for next steps. It is simple to present and it provides a level of security to prospects. Once they are in the meeting, they are able to discuss their concerns around your topic.

If you use a core value, you are tapping into something that is very meaningful to their occupation. That is the power of using the statement. But if your discussion then turns into the old sales rap about feature and function, you are going to be dismissed. The trick is to actually build a presentation that presents meaningful information, qualifies customer interest and preparedness, and creates a strategy for solving the problem that is met by what you are selling. As it pertains to our discussion in this chapter, it is important to remind yourself not to fall back into the sales process once you have worked so hard to remove yourself from it.

If you have engaged in an e-mail dialogue with a prospect and they have agreed to a briefing based on your core value, it will be entirely self-defeating to send them a preparation e-mail with a marketing slick of your solution! My motto is: once a meeting has been agreed upon, you should close until the briefing. You have slipped by their defenses. You don't need to alert them to your presence yet.

We have placed our conversation of developing Core-Value Declaration in the context of a group or entire company. But, if you are a sales or marketing associate, you don't need to wait for your managers to catch the vision of core value. You can integrate this principle into your cold calling or e-mail blasts immediately.

CHAPTER 5

Lose the Sales Stench

During the dot-com era, I had a close friend who had become the CEO of a struggling Internet start-up. Shawn had a brilliant knack for attracting venture-capital dollars. The company was very funded. But he could also see the writing on the wall. The market for Internet start-ups was slowing down. It was only a matter of time before the bubble popped. His financial backers began to put pressure on him to deliver revenue or produce a liquidity event.

Shawn had successfully directed his development team to morph its product into a unique set of portal-development software tools, but the market was slow and the investors were getting edgy. They were trying every avenue they could think of, but the revenues weren't picking up as had been expected.

As time went on, Shawn became increasingly concerned. He had heard about Blaire Group and my ability to get meetings with C-Level executives on demand. Shawn desperately needed sales, and he needed them quickly. So he contacted my office. Our conversation went something like this:

"Kraig, this is Shawn Carpenter; how goes it?"

"It's all good, Shawn. How's business?" I responded. I could hear the tension in his voice. Business had been good for Blaire Group, so I had a feeling that he was calling for help.

"Honestly, Kraig," he replied, "our product is sensational. But we are not getting deals as expected. I've got a feeling that some good reference accounts will get us moving like clockwork, but I'm having trouble initiating the conversations with our targeted buyers. We simply can't get any responses. I need my product reviewed quickly by the largest financial institutions in North America. Can you secure meetings with senior-level executives from that group of folks?"

I told him that I was confident a week of preparation would be all we would need to secure meetings with his prospects. Sure enough, after one week of deploying our *Must-React System,* we secured meetings with senior executives from Lehman Brothers, Citigroup, Merrill Lynch, Goldman Sachs, and the list goes on.

I vividly recall making contact with Bear Sterns' CEO, Jimmy Cayne, and coordinating the details of the meeting with his chief of staff. To this day, Shawn and I chuckle about our meeting in the Bear Sterns boardroom. In attendance were the CFO and four of his direct reports, the director of strategic planning and three people from his team, along with Bear Sterns' highest-ranking trading executive.

As Shawn was giving his PowerPoint presentation, the star trader executed a $50 million trade from his cell phone. Vinnie Dix must have received thirty cell phone calls during the course of that meeting. The star-studded brass of Bear Sterns had arrived to listen to the presentation of a small software company struggling to stay afloat. Why? Because we had avoided the pitfall of "smelling like sales" through two principles of *The Must-React System*: Enter the No-Product Zone and Less is More.

You have probably heard one of your co-workers saying "nobody wants to talk to salespeople." (Maybe you have thought this yourself!) This is especially true during prospecting. Good administrative assistants have been trained in smelling out a salesperson and sending them packing.

But the struggle to maintain relevance and attract new customers is felt most strongly by the senior executives in charge of providing a strategy for prospecting. You likely feel like my friend Shawn, even if your company isn't on the verge of losing venture-capital dollars. Every quarter, the earnings call comes around, and there must be a logical description of what is being done to attract new business. But competition is fierce. Shawn realized that if his company was going to make it for another round, they needed fast results, which meant that something needed to change in the way they introduced their company to prospective buyers.

The classic models of *Selling to Vito* and others have directed salespeople to place themselves in the center of the product zone. This is a great idea if you want to become irrelevant. If your sales call includes a declaration of how your company has saved other companies X dollars and you would like to talk about this great product you have, you are in the product zone. If you talk about your product on the first call, you might as well open your call with, "I'm Bill, and I hope to sell you something." Expect silence or a dial tone in response.

Below is a representative, ineffective script (either formal or informal) utilized by a typical sales professional attempting to schedule a meeting with a senior-executive target. While the script incorporates certain well-developed, fundamental selling techniques, it fails prima facie at delivering effective results for acquiring new prospect meetings with specified targets. It simply is not effective.

> **Sales:** *Hi, Jane. This is Bob Williams from Enterprise Software. Is Mr. Jones available?*
>
> **Admin:** *No, he isn't. May I take a message?*
>
> **Sales:** *I would like to schedule a thirty-minute meeting with him. Do you keep his calendar?*
>
> **Admin:** *Yes, I do. What is this regarding?*
>
> **Sales:** *I would like to introduce him to Enterprise Software and our suite of technology tools designed to enhance productivity and increase profits. Further, I'd like to show him how we increased Global Telecom's bottom-line financial results by 46% in a major business unit. Does he have availability during the week of (three weeks out)?*
>
> **Admin:** *A variety of no's … he doesn't meet with new vendors; call another person; I will leave him a message; send me an e-mail describing your company and the purpose of your meeting … all code language for no, no, no!*

More specifically, this dialogue fails for the following reasons:

- It is product-centric in its nature, and the culture resists product-centric messaging.
- It does not appeal to anyone's core values. In fact, it appeals to the administrator's abhorrences.
- It asked her to do something that she has been instructed not to do, which is to schedule a meeting with a new sales professional.
- She gets numerous, similar sales calls daily, and they all sound nearly identical to this one.

Further, the sales professional typically is ill-equipped to manage the following common objections without smelling like every other salesperson on the planet:

- Who is *ABC Company*?
- What does your company do?
- What is this meeting regarding?
- Can you send me an e-mail describing your request and I will discuss this with (target)?
- Are you a vendor?
- What is your product?

People are waiting for you to identify yourself as a salesperson. The new game of sales is hiding long enough to convince your prospects that they want a salesperson. The first step in that disguise process is avoiding the product zone. Marketing and sales efforts that are built around this tired old method are appealing only to those who have defined that they need the type of product that you are offering. But what about those prospects that have a project and have not yet identified their strategies for dealing with the problem?

You may feel that you only want to be speaking with people that have already determined they need a product like yours. But as we discussed in the introduction, companies already have vendors who provide your type of product. As there is a consolidation of vendors, there is a lower likelihood that they are going to seek out additional providers for any reason besides price points. Also, if they have already defined strategy that includes your product, they have probably received insight from one of your competitors. The gauntlet has already been set. And now you are playing according to your enemies' rules. As I talk with executives in sales, they always agree that they need to find prospects that have pain-points but have not yet determined what their strategy will be.

Since the goal is not to subject yourself to a sales cycle started by your competition but to find active need and produce a vision for your strategy, it is important to lose the sales stench by staying out of the product zone. This means removing any reference to product during any discussions or e-mails prior to a briefing. If you are pressed on the issue of whether or not your company sells any products for a certain problem, I suggest keeping the answer brief and emphasizing that although your company has a variety of products and services, your only intent is to schedule an executive briefing. Even when the briefing is being administered, I advise avoiding any discussion of product and services until the final slide of your PowerPoint deck. The name of the game is removing yourself from the sales cycle. This requires a commitment to avoiding product-centric discussions.

The principle of Enter the No-Product Zone short-circuits the listener's expectation that there is something being sold to them that they do not want. Instead of a product, he or she is being equipped with essential information specific for his or her industry and position. Core value replaces product on cold calls.

This practice is counterintuitive to most sales reps. Not only that, but many sales managers encourage product-centric discussions and meetings. There is a very strong school of thought that this is the only way to do sales. This is not only absolutely false, but it is soon to be totally outmoded. You may feel that you are conscious of this point. But I have yet to find a salesperson that properly follows this principle without training. Ask a co-worker to listen to your prospecting calls and keep track of all of the times you mention product. Then remove the product speech from your calls and evaluate the success rate. You will be surprised at the dramatic results.

The second is the problem of telling too much too soon. We call this the principle of Less is More. This is a common-sense practice in our daily lives. We don't normally tell a co-worker we just met about the deep dark secrets of our inner lives. It's too early in the relationship for that type of information. Prospecting is the same way. The purpose of prospecting is to set-up time for discussion. If an extensive discussion of your product is given too early, the prospect may think that he understands your offering. In actuality, he may be confused. I have also found that prospects who claim to have no interest in the type of product I am selling will open up and become more informative in the context of a briefing. I have been invited to several sales cycles through my ability to keep conversation to a minimum before having a format in which to speak at length.

Sales folks articulate the phrase "less is more" as if they are experts at this fundamental practice. Most of us have been exposed to the concept of less is more in Sales 101. Early in my selling career, this concept was highlighted in a variety of sales training programs that I experienced. The sad, sobering truth is that very few sales professionals have mastered the concept. Blaire Group recently completed a sales-audit analysis of sales professionals from the United States economy and ranked the least effective practices.[8]

Least Effective Practices

1. Sales professionals are much more inclined to speak than to listen. Few demonstrated an ability to "turn the tables" on any conversation and probe deeply to ascertain facts that are germane to advancing the sales cycle.

2. Most sales reps tend to overstate their own value proposition at the expense of understanding the motivation, plan, and desire that creates the logic for a tenable purchase rationale.

3. They are inclined to "speak ceaselessly" about their respective value propositions at the expense of exercising skill and craft at discovering the prospect's core values.

4. Verbal communications are haphazard and lack structure.

5. Sales professionals do not manage objections convincingly.

The information cited above shows that we have yet to truly master the simple concept of less is more. Instead of holding to a tightly scripted and well-planned prospecting practice, sales professionals are being "careless" and "haphazard" with their messaging. It is essential that we master this principle if we are to remove ourselves from the sales cycle.

When a person receives a call from someone they've never spoken with, his or her main goal becomes to end the call. There is an instinct that people do not want to talk to cold-callers. This may be the perfect person for your solution, but she doesn't know that and she isn't interested in finding out. There is a sense that people who call without being invited aren't worth talking to.

There are also other distractions in a person's office. She may be in the middle of another call or project when you reach her. She may be just overwhelmed by a variety of factors. It's your goal to bypass these distractions and move the conversation into a more comfortable space. If you have thirty minutes to an hour of secured time, you can be sure that your communication will be more likely to be absorbed, and you will be able to truly qualify the needs and interest of the prospect. Neither of these is likely to happen on an initial call. So extensive talking is not only meaningless; it can be destructive.

The principle of Less is More is also counterintuitive. We tend to think that if we explain ourselves, we will be better understood. This is untrue during prospecting efforts. As we mentioned earlier, you need to move the conversation into a different space in order to truly have your prospects' attention. On the first call, their attitude is to eliminate you as quickly as possible. By keeping your message as short as possible, you avoid possible objections that might be raised and you keep the focus on your objective: scheduling a next step.

Less is More applies to e-mails and presentations as well as calling. Every prospecting e-mail I have read has been obnoxiously long. If a prospect actually reads an e-mail from an unknown sender, they first scan the size of the e-mail to see if they have time to read it. If the e-mail *appears* to be several pages in length, they will disregard the entire content! Even if the most pertinent content was placed in the introduction (which is not always the case), the prospect would not be exposed to it because he or she is overwhelmed by the amount of possible information in an e-mail that he or she has no interest in receiving.

The other red flag for marketing and sales e-mails is being rich in pictures or attachments. These are warning signs for recipients that this is a solicitation. Our job is to avoid looking like every other salesperson in the world. We don't want our e-mails hitting the junk box. And we don't want them getting skimmed and then trashed.

Less is More solves this e-mail problem. The normal prospecting e-mail I build for a client is only two or three sentences in length. It contains the Core Value Declaration and requests a meeting for discussion. It doesn't alert itself as a sales or marketing request because it doesn't contain a variety of rich media elements or PDF attachments. Instead, it removes itself from the sales process by keeping the information to a minimum instead of a maximum. If people want more information, they are required to get it from you. Once this happens, you have gotten a reaction from the prospect, and your likelihood of scheduling your briefing has been increased. Popular e-mail marketing sites boast of sometimes a 1% response rate to their e-mail blasts. My *Must-React* e-mails have received a 19% response rate. This is primarily because we employ the principles of Core Value Statement and Less is More.

When I evaluate sales presentations, I feel sorry for everyone who has ever seen them. I have yet to find a presentation that does not feel like it believes more is more. There is significantly more text than is necessary on the slides. There is more information than we need in the presentation. And there is more product-centric nonsense than the customers can stomach. Enough with the slide of your top customer. Stop including a long history of your company. We certainly don't need to know anything about your personal history on a slide. You can pepper these into your presentation. But they are seasoning. Use them sparingly. Remember: until the final slide of your introductory presentation, you are removing yourself from the sales cycle. Keeping the principle of Less is More in the introductory presentation will keep your prospect engaged and interested in performing a next step.

CHAPTER 6

Know Your Enemy

Tim Stassi was the co-founder of a telecommunications software company named The Angeles Group. After many years of corporate success, he and his partner decided that a sale of the company would be in the best interest of all of the shareholders.

Tim directed his executive team to prepare the company to be sold. They employed a team of investment bankers and mergers and acquisitions (M&A) consultants. After several months, the sale of the company had not progressed to the satisfaction of the board. And although Tim was able to run a successful software company, he was unable to generate interest for purchase from other companies. Large sums of money were being spent on consultants, but it might as well have been thrown in a black hole. The sale was going nowhere.

Tim reached out to my office. He was inquiring as to whether our *Must-React System* could be applied to assist The Angeles Group in its search to find an acquiring partner. As we usually specialized strictly in sales consulting at a product level, we hesitated to give a definitive answer. Instead, I flew to L.A. to meet with Tim and his engineering partner. We spent a considerable amount of time determining whether this was a project that was ripe for *Must-React*. I felt confident that selling a company was just another sales process just like any other. Tim and his partner agreed to move forward.

I helped Tim's executive team in a lot of areas: I created a viable defense for valuation; I cleaned up some of the financial reporting; and I developed a target list of possible acquiring partners that consisted of CEOs from a variety of large and medium-sized corporations. (In our language, I was creating a Core-Value Declaration and defining a target list.)

I remember Tim telling me, "Kraig, if you can secure meetings with three CEOs from this top-twenty list, I will be thrilled." With my marching orders in hand, I flew back to Chicago to execute our first *Must-React* M&A campaign.

Why had I proceeded on this new venture with such confidence after meeting with Tim and his partner? Because I realized that although they had hired a team of "big brains" to sell the company, they had neglected a key form of leverage in gaining access to executives: the principle of Power Responds to Power. Tim was the founder and CEO of his company. That was a claim to power that only a small number of people could make. I knew that if we built a message around the power of Tim's position, we could meet with other CEOs.

My call script to our CEO targets was constructed 100% according to *The Must-React System*. Since I knew that I would likely be connected to administrative assistants, and because I wanted the target to directly hear my message, I would ask the admin to connect me to the target's voice mail the moment she picked up. (I usually do not recommend this, but it made most sense for this assignment.) Upon reaching the voice mail "beep," I stated the following:

> *Hi Mr. Johnson, this is Kraig Kleeman with Blaire Group. I have been retained by the CEO and board of directors at The Angeles Group to assist them with some strategic-planning issues. I have advised that they consider a variety of options, including joint venture opportunities, or possibly even consolidation with a few select organizations, of which your company is one. I would like to have dialogue with you on this subject at your earliest convenience. Please contact me at 312.555.1212. Thank you so much.*

The phones started ringing! Though he was in Europe, one CEO target returned my call within twenty minutes. Meetings with CEOs of targeted buyers for The Angeles Group were being scheduled rapidly.

Within two weeks, we had secured meetings with *all twenty of our targets*, and within forty-five days, we had three letters of intent. Ultimately, Tim Stassi and his engineering partner sold the company at a valuation that was amazing. Why couldn't the investment bankers and M&A consultants succeed with this project? Sadly, they did not understand, nor did they deploy, the leverage of Power Responds to Power.

There are a variety of leverage techniques to use when building a strategy to attack net-new customers. The technique you use will be based entirely upon the person you are hoping to contact. So if you haven't established a Core-Value Declaration and a target list, go back to Chapter 3 and complete that first. If you have established whom you want to talk to, you need to figure out if the strategy of Power Responds to Power or Peer Reacts to Peer will be more effective. There is a different technique if you are calling for a CIO and you reach his assistant than if you are calling for a project manager and you reach him directly. You will also leverage the conversation with the CIO's administrative assistant differently depending on his or her temperament.

When you are calling on senior-level executives in your accounts, there is an understood power arrangement. They have it and you don't. A C-Level executive doesn't want to take a meeting with an account manager. He has meetings with other C-level executives. His administrative assistant understands this and acts accordingly. He or she has been instructed to keep salespeople off the executive's calendar. He is inundated by requests from salespeople for introductory meetings. Remember, in a week, average executives:

- spend 66% of their time out of the office,
- spend 35% of their time with customers,
- receive 360 pieces of mail,
- receive 240 phone calls,
- receive 143 voice mail messages,
- and receive 288 e-mail messages.

Ugh! With this type of clamoring, most C-Level executives are harder to meet with than Bono in a bar full of fans. But you can use the leverage of power in your favor by attributing the source of the meeting to the SVP, EVP, or even CEO of your company.

This does not mean that you should "flex-up" on the phone and show off your verbal muscles. Rather, this simply means that in our culture, people respond to authority. If you are calling on behalf of your CEO, suddenly there is a mandate from another position of power that this meeting must happen! Imagine the difference when you state that you have been instructed by your chief officer to schedule a meeting with your prospect! The prospect is appealed to meet because another person in power is requesting a meeting with them.

The principle of Power Responds to Power removes you from the sales cycle by making your meetings appear to be focused on that specific executive. Presumably, CEOs don't have time to meet with every one of their customers and prospects. That's why they have hired sales and marketing teams. The very fact that the meeting is being arranged on behalf of a senior executive gives prospects a feeling that they are specifically being invited. It removes the scent of mass marketing and brings the power of executive force to bear on them.

This principle also puts any gatekeeper in a precarious situation. We know that they have been instructed to keep salespeople off of executive calendars. But what instruction have they received about calls from other executives? I have literally been able to have administrative assistants pull executives out of board meetings or give me personal contact information based on this principle.

It is simple to employ this principle in your prospecting practices. When you are drafting a calling script or an e-mail, simply begin every one with "Our founder and CEO, Mr. Bob Thomson, has requested I schedule a meeting with you ..." Just by utilizing the words "our founder and CEO," the conversation has immediate credibility with the administrative assistant. When she hears the phrase words "CEO" and "organize a meeting," she must react. Compare that to the typical script used by sales professionals:

> *Hi Jane. My name is Robert Williams with XYZ Corporation. I would like to schedule a meeting with Mr. Johnson to introduce him to our ABC product suite and share with him how we saved Zurich Insurance $3million in its first year of application of our technology.*

Jane receives forty requests daily inviting Mr. Williams to a sales call. But how many invitations does she get centered on a request from a CEO? Jane will react to this request. She must react.

Some people feel uncomfortable using this method. They feel that if they propose a meeting scheduled on behalf of their CEO, the CEO should actually be in attendance. I have used this principle thousands of times personally, and I have rarely encountered a problem. By the time the meeting actually happens, prospects are usually rushing from one event to another. They don't have time to review every appointment they've made. Usually, they don't even remember that it was our CEO who requested the meeting. When I begin our presentation, I simply assume that I am the person the CEO has requested present on his behalf. If the prospect is obviously bothered, or even threatens to terminate the meeting because the CEO hasn't arrived, I inform him or her that the CEO requested that I schedule and present the meeting on his or her behalf.

You don't need to use the CEO title. If you have determined your target and core value, you can use whatever title would be most appealing to your prospect. It may be an industry expert or a director of compliance. Whoever it is, you can use the leverage of her title to break down gatekeepers and schedule your qualification briefing. Once you have engaged the briefing, you are able to shift gears and make suggestions as to who should be involved in future meetings. The essential point when prospecting is to Remove Yourself from the Sales Cycle. Power Responds to Power accomplishes this goal.

When populating trade shows, I advise using the title of your highest-ranking participant to invite trade show attendees to meetings at the trade show. At the very least, prospects will turn down an official meeting in favor of attending your booth. But often times, you will be able to schedule several one-on-one discussions in the middle of a largely populated event. These in-depth discussions are more fruitful than the elevator pitches that are so typical of those large events.

When performing trade show follow-up, you can reference your request for a meeting at the trade show and inform the prospect that your director was intent on speaking with them at the show and has requested a follow-up meeting.

I advise always using the technique of Power Responds to Power in your initial calls. If you have never spoken with a prospect before, you need to call with the assumption that they are going to take a meeting. Using the principle of Power Responds to Power bolsters this attitude. However, if this technique is not working, you can switch to the principle of Peer Reacts to Peer.

Peer Reacts to Peer works because we react to people with whom we feel share a common bond. You use this by emphasizing your role as a subordinate to someone in power just as your contact is. You may try to draw a similarity between your relationship with your CEO or other senior executive and the administrative assistant's relationship to their executive. Emphasizing the fact that you have no choice in the matter but you simply must schedule time with the target because you are being ordered to by your boss can make the administrative assistant feel like they need to help you.

While we are on the topic of using titles to schedule meetings, we should discuss a topic I call "masking." Masking means changing your title based on the target you are attempting to contact. Titles and job descriptions are given by companies to explain your relationship to other people in your company. They do not accurately describe your relationship with your prospect. If you are an "account manager" in Chicago-land and you sell primarily to banks, you may want to refer to yourself as a "financial services specialist/analyst". You can adjust the title based on your client base. Once again, what we are trying to do is to accurately depict the relationship between ourselves and clients in such a way that they will feel more inclined to meet with us. You can use Power Responds to Power and avoid the product zone all day long, but if you go around telling people you are an account manager, you are still going to smell like a sales rat.

CHAPTER 7

Control the Call

Three years ago, I was brought into an enterprise software company to build an inside sales team. I began hiring for the team just after Christmas. We wanted ten young people to begin the 2005 sales year for the company. Due to some human resources snafus, we weren't able to make all of our hires. When we returned from the Christmas and New Year's break, I got a call from an old friend of mine. His son had recently graduated from college and was looking to break into the sales scene. I had known this young man since he was a small child, but I hadn't been in touch with him personally for several years. I had no idea what type of ability he would have.

Our goal for the team was to have people with five years or more of sales experience. We had to get this project off the ground fast and show results if we wanted to stay funded. But I decided that hiring Len was a good idea. His father was a great sales guy, and I had a feeling that the apple didn't fall far from the tree. What's more, I tend to prefer working with people that haven't been exposed to a lot of the negative sales training. At times, it seems easier to teach people the elements of my system if they aren't already bound up with bad habits.

Right out of the gate, the team was performing as expected. In our first week, we had C-level meetings with a good cross section of America's finest companies. The members of the group were each averaging twenty briefings per month!

After just three months, Len began scheduling meetings at one of America's top ten banks. We had been trying to sell this particular account for years, but we were stuck in the information technology group. There was a gatekeeper for our product that would never introduce us to other areas of the company or give us meetings with the CIO. If the salesperson tried to go around the gatekeeper, he would throw a fit! However, the gatekeeper didn't know about Len. So that's the way we kept it. We decided to let Len continue calling the account until our gatekeeper yanked on our leash.

It wasn't long before Len had scheduled a briefing with a senior vice president from another business unit in the bank. They had a project to present their retail customers' statements to the Web. Len scheduled several additional meetings for our sales team to go and build the project without our contacts in IT knowing. Within a little less than a year, the deal closed for more than a million dollars!

Len was excited about the commissions and the respect gained from such a high visibility account. But the really exciting part of the story is that he was only twenty-one when this happened. Not many people his age could have claimed to originate a million-dollar deal their first year in the business, much less schedule the introductory meetings that led to that deal.

The reason Len was able to discover this deal was that he had been thoroughly trained in *The Must-React System*. It was through The System that he learned how to control the call, even if it was a top executive at one of the largest banks in the country!

How many times have you had a call end by the prospect telling you what was going to happen next? If this is the case, I consider the call a failure. I am the person with an objective for the call, not them. How is it that they got what they wanted from the discussion and not me? There are several ways to avoid this pitfall of cold calling and to ensure that you control the call.

It is essential that you are the person in control during any prospecting event. Time and time again, I am astonished at how little control is brought to a call, e-mail, or presentation by the sales professionals involved. Often, there seems to be no strategy behind the interaction. It is apparent that they have not properly prepared for the event. I have seen some people just unaware of their schedules, so they are unable to commit to a hard date on the phone with a prospect. This boggles my mind! Why are you calling people for a meeting if you don't know when you can meet? Or, more commonly, a salesperson will be presenting his company's presentation and it feels as if he has never seen the slides before. He's reading the content directly from the page, unable to answer simple questions, and the content is unsystematic with no central thrust. Plain and simple: you are the quarterback in this game called sales. If you don't know what's going on, your prospect certainly won't. You need to get control of the call.

While in college, I was impacted by the Middle East peace treaty brokered by President Jimmy Carter. I was coming to grips with my own worldview, which included issues of great import such as world peace, complex social injustices, racial discrimination and reverse racial discrimination, and the centrality and role of human government, as well as individual spirituality.

The Arab-Israeli conflict had become an intense focus of interest in my developing mind. Israeli Prime Minister Menachem Begin and Egyptian President Anwar Sadat had recently entered into a high-stakes gamble when they signed the pact, which was designed to foster peace and stability in the region. It was a classic "land for peace" deal. Though he did not know it at the time, President Carter was on his way to win a Nobel Peace Prize for his amazing efforts!

As a young idealist with great concern for the security of Israel, I followed these events with insatiable scrutiny. Amazed at the outcome, I was determined to personally congratulate Prime Minister Begin for his outstanding courage in the face of significant resistance from the hard-liners amongst Israel's parliament, the Knesset. One day, over lunch, I told several of my friends of how I was really hoping to speak with the prime minister. From that point on, my wish became a running joke with my friends. They laughed about my total ignorance of politics. They told me I was totally naïve if I thought I was actually going to have the chance to speak with him. When I boldly stated that I wasn't going to *have* a chance to meet with him, I was going to *create* one, they became even more enthused. We decided that I would attempt to reach Begin later that evening.

When I first started calling, I only knew one thing: Begin would have a staff of people that were trained to deal with matters on his behalf. They would be attempting to lead and direct me to anyone besides Begin. If I wanted to speak with the prime minister, I was going to need to be the one who directed the call. The moment I let the conversation get out of my control would be the moment I lost. And so, over a period of thirty minutes, I spoke with a variety of different members of his personal staff. Forcefully, I explained to each of them that I intended to speak with the prime minister.

On that fateful night in 1980, from my dorm room at Judson College, I secured a private telephone meeting with Israeli Prime Minister Begin, congratulating him for his efforts and eventual success at signing the remarkable peace pact with Egypt. Imagine, a second-year student attending a little-known private college in Chicago's suburbs conducting a "congratulatory" phone call with a sovereign nation's prime minister! There was an enormous buzz on campus. "Who will

Kleeman get on the phone next? How does he do that?" Little did I know that in my adult future, I would be leading workshops training a whole host of professionals how to Control the Call.

So, why do so many people lose control of their prospecting activity, and how can you gain control and get meetings with people you never thought possible? Many salespeople lose control of their prospecting activity, be it cold calling, e-mail, or presentations, because they do not have a clearly defined goal for their activity. In *The Must-React System*, we are always driving every prospecting event toward the safe space of a qualification briefing. But I have trained hundreds of salespeople who would block out several days for prospecting in their month just because they knew they needed to. They might send out several e-mails to new prospects or make several hundred phone calls. But when I would ask them what their next step for this activity was, very few could articulate a response. Many times, they were just responding to direction from their boss to send a customer success story to all of their accounts. They seemed to assume that their prospects would come back to them begging for an onsite meeting. This passive prospecting is leaving the control in the hands of the prospect. They will use it. But it will be to their advantage and not yours. They may respond, requesting more information or letting you know that they will forward your content to the appropriate person in their company. But who is going to take the initiative to schedule a meeting from information that has been forwarded by a co-worker?

The fact is that People Require Leadership. The first principle to understand when controlling the call is that People Require Leadership. I don't care if you are talking about the CEO of a Fortune 500 company or the director of operations at a regional bank. The plain truth is that most people both want and need leadership. Leadership in prospecting is about proactively guiding the contact to your desired goal.

I often hear salespeople asking the prospect what he or she thinks the next step should be in a sales cycle. If the sales cycle was a football game, next steps would be the plays called. Any salesperson worth her salt should be calling the plays. To let the customer choose the next step is like the quarterback allowing the defense to choose his next play. It's a crazy idea when you think about it that way. But that's what is happening during sales calls every day.

Prospects are not normally professional buyers. Let's assume that they do want to buy your product. They do not have a strategy in mind for how they are going to achieve that goal. They will make suggestions about what the next steps should be, but it will just be the first thing that comes to mind. They are not proactively trying to progress your deal. You, however, are a professional seller. From the first contact to the moment that ink hits paper, you need to provide leadership and guidance to your buyer.

Taking leadership on a call requires that you maintain a confident presence through your statements and instructions. Most people will either give you their direction or follow yours, depending on the timing and delivery. At each and every point, you need to have several next steps in your mind so that you can provide leadership to your contact. When you provide leadership, you Use Commanding Statements, you Close Early, you realize Deadlines Really Work, and you give alternative close dates.

The primary way to provide leadership during prospecting is to Use Commanding Statements. Commanding statements are clear instructions given to the prospect telling them what they need to do. You can see the difference between asking for a meeting whenever they are available and telling a prospect that you "need to schedule this meeting by the end of the week." Commanding statements depend on next steps. If you don't know what your next step is, you can't command it. So figure out a three-step process for each of your prospecting events. If you are cold calling, think of three possible next steps for your call. You might choose a Web meeting to discuss industry research, an onsite meeting to introduce your company, or you might qualify enough information on your initial call and decide that a product demonstration is your next step. Alternatively, if you are scheduling qualification briefings, you need to have several prepared next steps. Often, I will close for a deeper-dive meeting to discuss specific interests, a product demonstration, or an onsite trial use of the product. What you are closing for will depend on your industry and product. Regardless of what the event is, you must have it defined and be able to command your prospects' attention.

What do *Commanding Statements* sound like? Consider the difference between these two cold calls:

> **Mr. Prospect**: *Hello?*
> **Kraig:** *Good morning, Bob, this is Kraig Kleeman from Blaire Group. I'm new to your territory and wanted to take a moment to introduce myself and our company.*

> **Mr. Prospect**: *I'm really too busy to speak with new vendors, Kraig.*
> *I've got to go.*
> **Kraig**: *I understand this is a busy time of year. Stay well Bob.*

To the untrained ear, this may sound like a polite call. The prospect is too busy to talk. Instead of forcing the information down his throat, I decided to wait until he had time to pay attention to my information. But let's see how it would work with commanding statements employed.

> **Mr. Prospect:** *Hello?*
> **Kraig:** *Good morning, Bob; this is Kraig Kleeman from Blaire Group. I need to schedule thirty minutes with you for a briefing on increasing pipeline productivity. What is your availability for Thursday of this week?*
> **Mr. Prospect:** *Thursday is booked. I'm just super busy this week, Kraig.*
> **Kraig:** *I understand. Why don't we look at next week? Next Wednesday at 3:00 is available. Let's plan on speaking then. I'll call you at your office.*
> **Mr. Prospect:** *I think that will work.*
> **Kraig:** *I know you're busy, Bob. I'll e-mail a confirmation to you. We'll talk to you Wednesday.*

You can see how in the second call, I commanded a meeting immediately. Because I made a direct inquiry for a meeting time on Thursday instead of waiting for Mr. Prospect to guide the call, he was in the position of responding to me. When he revealed he was booked for the week, I immediately moved on and commanded a date the following week. Since Bob was in a reactive frame of mind, he simply told me he was available. I then closed the call until I could have his full attention.

When I teach the principle of People Require Leadership, I tell people to close the cold call as soon as possible. Once again, this requires a clear understanding of what the next step is. The example we have been using is calling for a meeting. The script I write for cold calls always includes a close for a meeting in the first or second sentence. If there is a rebuttal, I give an answer and immediately close for the meeting again. Often, I will use a stronger close than before. If I opened by simply closing for the meeting, I might close for a meeting tomorrow afternoon this time. Let's evaluate an actual e-mail exchange. A member of my staff sent the following:

> Bob,
> Our Founder and CEO, Kraig Kleeman, has instructed me to schedule a thirty-minute briefing with you on the topic of "predictable prospecting." Please advise your best availability to meet.

"Bob" responded.

> I don't think I know Kraig. Please forward some information on the content of this meeting.
> Bob

We responded.

> Bob,
> This briefing is the result of eighteen months of industry research conducted by Mr. Kleeman's personal research group. He is currently available to meet Friday morning at 10:00 AM CDT. I have included a bridge line for our meeting.

The prospect responded that he was available. This is not an isolated event. The key in this case was constantly focusing on the close.

You will notice that we basically ignored Bob's request for more information. We told him it was a research briefing and then we returned to our goal for the e-mail, which was scheduling a meeting. Imagine what would have happened if, instead of closing early, we had engaged in a long exchange of information with Bob. I have seen people actually send a soft copy of the presentation they were hoping to give. At that point, you haven't exchanged information. You've given it away. There is no reason for the prospect to meet with you anymore. Avoid giving away more than you intend by keeping your responses short and focusing on the close.

The next part of keeping control during prospecting is giving a deadline for achieving a goal. This is part of what I call creating a sense of urgency. I have literally received callbacks in minutes by using this technique. It works like this: whenever you need something from your prospect, whether it's a simple call back or a meeting, you tell them when you need it. A classic voice mail I use combines this with the principle of Less is More. I will simply tell the prospect, "Bill, this is Kraig from Chicago. I need to reach you by 3:00 PM. Call me as soon as possible at my number." Alternatively, if I am scheduling a meeting, I will tell them that we need to meet or that we need to schedule the meeting by a certain date. More often than not, they comply, and I have controlled when the meeting occurred. If I had left that decision in their hands, they may have pushed it out a month or more. You can combine this principle with Peer Reacts to Peer if you need to put additional pressure on an administrative assistant or a gatekeeper. If you are not getting the response you need or you feel that the assistant is simply delaying scheduling your meeting, you can simply tell them that your boss has requested a status update on their account by 4:00 and he is insistent that a meeting be scheduled. The purpose of this principle is to get the contact to feel the same urgency you do for scheduling a meeting.

Alternative Close Dates is a classic prospecting tool that is too often overlooked. It is a simple way of maintaining control on the call by giving multiple options to the prospect that work for you. When closing for the date of a meeting, you may ask the prospect whether she prefers to meet on Tuesday or Thursday of the following week. This gives her the impression that she is making a choice about the issue, but in reality, she is only working within the restrictions you have given her. Either option that she chooses will work for you.

You can control the call. We have discussed how employing the principles of People Require Leadership, Use Commanding Statements, Deadlines Really Work, and Offer Alternative Close Dates can give you more control in your prospecting efforts. In the next section of the book, we are going to discuss how the different principles of The System can be applied to your prospecting process.

CHAPTER 8

Build a Message

The Must-React System is a prospecting methodology. It is designed to create demand from new clients. We have discussed why the old way of sales has ceased to be attractive to prospects, and we have laid out the elements of The System. But reading about the principles and seeing them in action are two very different things. I have tried to paint a picture for you by telling some of the stories that The System has produced. In the following chapter, we are going to provide some hands-on information about how to build a call script, wage an e-mail battle, and create *Must-React* presentation messaging.

Building a Core Value

In Chapter 4, we discussed the importance of core value. This is the foundation of any messaging type (cold-calling script, e-mail, or presentation). We'll start by showing how we have established core values for some of our clients.

To build a core value declaration, it is helpful to start with a rubric. This is a topic or phrase that you can use that will help you think productively about the message you are trying to deliver. The rubric we will use for this exercise is: "top operating issues facing _____." When you are trying to build a core value, insert the industry you are targeting in the first blank and the title you are targeting in the second. For example, if you have "top banking operating issue facing senior vice presidents," that is the first part of your core value. But the catch is that the statement always ends in a colon. It needs you to add some color to the end. So we might come up with something like "top banking issues facing SVP of operations: controlling corporate content."

Core values statements that we have built when the target is a CEO appeal to his or her goals for quarter-over-quarter profits. We know that the primary task of any chief officer to is to benefit his or her board and stockholders. The name of the game for the CEO is client retention and new client acquisition.

If you are writing core value for a CIO, you would probably be tempted to boast about product functionality, but if you are staying out of the product zone, that isn't an option. A core value declaration we built for a CIO was "strategies for global content consolidation." Another popular value in today's IT environment is "strategies for vendor rationalization in a global environment."

Perhaps you are targeting accounts payable. You might start with our rubric of "top operating issues facing accounts payable managers." The issues in this case would be gaining lower rates from vendors and reducing the amount of late payments being made. One of values that I wrote which was highly successful was "benchmarking business process through accounts payable."

When I was working with a software company, that made a fantastic tool for agent portal. But regardless of the ability of the tool, the salespeople were unable to get meetings to begin discussions with prospects. The product in itself was unable to create appeal. We created a core value that was able to by pass the defenses of prospective buyers. In the insurance industry, we know that agent turnover poses a huge concern to agency, marketing, and sales executives. The value is then "optimizing agent retention and productivity." Once we implemented the *Must-React* message, we were able to give this product the visibility it deserved by producing hundreds of meetings with potential buyers. We led with the messaging and then brought the product in after the prospect had been qualified.

For the legal, corporate counsel, and compliance officer, we know that there is an incredible pressure for corporate compliance in our post-Enron era. There are also issues of records retention, litigation preparedness, regulatory affairs, etc. There are several possible core values that could be written with these issues in mind. One that we have used with our clients has been "optimizing process efficiencies—corporate records and control." Or "records retention, litigation preparedness, and regulatory compliance." This has proven to be very effective.

How to Write a *Must-React* Calling Script

Here, we talk about how to write a script and how to be prepared for objections. We will use examples from past scripts and discuss the differences between traditional cold-calling scripts and a *Must-React* script. The *Must-React* calling script builds on every element of *The Must-React System*. We will discuss the way these work as we are building the script.

The primary goal of every *Must-React* script is to schedule a qualification briefing. As we discussed in Chapter 4, prospects feel uneasy on the phone with a person they have never met. By moving the call immediately to the qualification briefing, we will be able to put the prospect at ease and in turn, they will be more willing to share information with us.

Remember, we are trying to remove ourselves from the sales cycle. The goal of this calling script is to minimize the appeal of product and solution and to maximize the importance of delivering messages that contain your customers' core values. In order to do this, we need to build several responses to the standard objections from a prospect or administrative assistant. We want to keep the sense of urgency high and the focus on the core value. We must at all times avoid any product jargon or reference to product, even when describing the company you work for. There are several stock questions that a world-class cold caller needs to have pre-built responses for: Who are you? What do you want? Are you a vendor? Is this a sales call? Let's start by building a script for dealing with administrative assistants. The first step is to avoid the admin altogether. We would prefer to have her transfer us to the prospect directly.

> **Sales**: *Hi, is Bob in?*
> **Admin**: *No, he is not.*
> **Sales**: *When will he be available?*
> **Admin**: *What is this regarding?*

In most cases, we will end up being screened by the admin. Fortunately, this process is fairly common and there are a few moves that we can anticipate. The first is that she will try and disqualify our meeting by identifying it as a sales call. That is what is going on in our current script. We need to have several responses memorized that will short circuit her sense that we are salespeople. Here are a couple possible answers:

> **Sales:** *I need to schedule a thirty-minute briefing with Bob. Do you keep his calendar?*
> Or:
> **Sales:** *I'm Kraig from Blaire Group. Our founder and CEO, Mr. Brad Jenkins, asked me to organize a meeting with Bob. Do you keep his calendar?*
> **Admin**: *Yes, I do, but I need more information.*

In our two responses, we varied the principles of Less is More and Power Responds to Power. In the first response, we are keeping the admin on her toes by giving enough information to answer her question but then moving directly to the close by asking for calendar information. In the second, we employ Power Responds to Power to throw her off the sales scent. In many cases, we are able to close for a meeting at this point in the call. But let's assume the admin responded as above. How would we react? At this point, many salespeople would launch into stories about their company or a story about how much they have saved a customer that is in a similar industry. This is self-defeating, as the admin is trying to smell out any salespeople at this point. We will avoid this trap by restating our original position and then offering alternative close dates.

> **Sales**: *I'm the special assistant to our founder and CEO, Mr. Brad Jenkins. He asked me to schedule a thirty-minute meeting with Bob. I plan to accomplish this by the end of the next week. I currently have availability on Wednesday or Thursday. Do either of these days work for him/her?*

Instead of asking for more information, the admin may have asked:

> **Admin**: *Who is Blaire Group?*

In this case, we need to maintain the posture of losing the sales stench. The traditional technique of telling her of our long, proud history distributing sales management products is going to get us transferred to the vendor box. Our chances of securing a meeting will be totally extinguished. Instead, *Must-React*

Messaging will craft a message that will give her enough information to combat her question, but not enough to position this as a sales call.

> **Sales**: *We are a global organization. We have engagements with sixty of the fortune 100. Our CEO, Mr. Jenkins, specifically asked me to schedule a meeting with Bob. Would either of those days work for him/her?*
> **Admin**: *What is this meeting in regards to? What is the meeting about?*

The admin on our call is pretty sharp. She is going to make sure that this call from a CEO is legitimate. We need to be very careful how we position the meeting. The principle of Less is More is critical when speaking with a gatekeeper of any sort. Extra information is only going to help them block you from your goal. Our response is going to emphasize the core value declaration we have constructed.

> **Sales**: *Mr. Jenkins' personal research team recently completed an eighteen-month study analyzing every aspect of the (**INSERT CORE VALUES STATEMENT**), and he asked me to specifically set up a thirty-minute meeting with Bob to review the results of this study. Would either of those days work for him/her?*
> **Admin**: *Can you send an e-mail regarding this topic?*

A classic line! Prospects will often request more information to be sent so they can distribute it to the correct people. In reality, this is a push-off. I advise pushing back on this request. If they really want more information, why don't they just schedule a meeting? In this script, we are going to refuse to forward information.

> **Sales**: *This is proprietary information that can only be delivered via Web conference.*

More often than not, the admin will tell you that she can't schedule a meeting without more information. At this point, you can simply tell her that this information is to be reviewed by your prospect personally and have her direct you to a time when

"Bob" can be reached directly or to give you a mobile number or e-mail address that he can be contacted at. You can add urgency to this by stating that your CEO has mandated that this meeting occur before the end of the week.

Another strong-arm maneuver is:

> **Admin:** *Is Mr. (prospect name) aware of this?*

The question behind the question is, "Was this meeting requested?" This question has been developed in a culture where un-requested meetings are unwanted meetings. This could cripple an old cold-calling script. But the *Must-React* script understands that it is not selling a sales call. It is scheduling a briefing based around the target's core values. Why would they not want to attend? We respond by stifling their question and then providing leadership.

> **Sales**: *I don't know. What I do know is that we are dealing with complex schedules on both sides. Let's work together to find a common placeholder and then we can circle back and confirm.*

I often advise clients to use placeholders as a way to schedule a meeting through a hesitant admin, the reason being that when you are in a cold-call battle, the admin is on the offensive. He or she is bound and determined to stop your meeting. But if you can get a placeholder on the calendar, a short call or e-mail later in the week to confirm a previously arranged meeting will be easily approved.

Another possible reaction might be:

> **Admin**: *I'll have to check with Bob and get back to you.*

This is simply a last-ditch effort to keep from scheduling your briefing. The admin can no longer think of any excuses for not scheduling the meeting. Now she has to check with her boss. This is a reversal of the principle of Peer Reacts to Peer. The admin is trying to say that she reports to this prospect and there is no way that she can schedule a meeting on his behalf. This is a total smoke screen. Administrative assistants schedule meetings on behalf of the people they work for all the time. But she/he can't think of anything to say; she knows a reaction is needed; and not wanting to take the responsibility, she places it on her boss. This is when we employ the principle Peer Responds to Peer.

> **Sales**: *Here is my dilemma; I have been mandated by Mr. Jenkins to schedule a meeting with Mr. (prospect name). When will Mr. (prospect name) be available?*

By placing the onus of the briefing back on our CEO, you do two things. You remove yourself from the situation. You are creating the perception that you, personally, have no choice in the matter. It is something that has been mandated by your CEO. You must schedule the meeting. You also maintain the same story you have been trying to sell through the use of Power Responds to Power. If you were to cripple at this point, it would make the entire appeal to the CEO meeting seem like a farce.

> **Admin**: *I cannot schedule a meeting without Mr. (prospect name's) prior consent. I will take your name and number and call you back, or send me an e-mail with an outline and we will get back to you.*

If the call reaches this point, I would try putting the admin on hold for a few seconds. Silence will play to your advantage. If needed, I will use this technique and then return to the call suggesting a placeholder for later in the month. I will ask her to "pencil it in" on his calendar until it is officially approved. Then I will call back in the next twenty-four hours to confirm. By then, the conflict of the call has worn down, and it is likely that the admin will not remember our exchange. She will simply see the placeholder on the calendar and confirm the meeting.

If the admin won't put a placeholder on the calendar, I will ask to be placed into the prospect's voice mail. If the voice mail to the prospect is built around the principle of Less is More, Power Responds to Power, and Core Value, you will see a high response rate. A typical voice mail will be:

> **Sales:** *Hello, Bob, my name is Kraig and I'm special assistant to our founder and CEO, Mr. Brad Jenkins, who asked me to schedule a meeting. Please call me at (your call back number). Thanks so much.*

Many of these phrases can be easily adjusted when you are speaking directly to a prospect instead of an admin. An additional technique that we did not discuss in admin script was an appeal to the core value. Consider the following:

> **Bob:** *Hello, this is Bob.*
> **Sales:** *Bob, this is Kraig Kleeman with Blaire Group, and I'm calling to schedule a thirty-minute briefing with you. Is Thursday or Friday a better day to meet?*
> **Bob:** *I don't take sales calls.*
> **Sales:** *Bob, this isn't a sales call. This is an information briefing on the topic of client retention and new client acquisition. I have been directed by the office of our CEO to schedule this meeting with you directly.*
> **Bob:** *I'm not interested in meeting.*
> **Sales:** *Bob, are you still the CEO of Halifax, Inc.?*
> **Bob:** *Yes.*
> **Sales:** *And is the topic of client retention and new client acquisition germane to you?*
> **Bob:** *Yes, but I'm very busy.*
> **Sales:** *That's exactly why you need to take this meeting. Our research group has compiled information from an eighteen-month project commissioned by our CEO's office to present to other CEOs such as yourself. This thirty-minute briefing will feature the highlights of our research. What is your availability on Thursday?*
> **Bob:** *I can do thirty minutes at 9:00 AM.*
> **Sales:** *That will be enough time for our presentation. I will forward the details to your assistant. Bye for now.*

Did you see how we appealed to the core value declaration when the meeting was initially turned down? Instead of offering to call back later or forward some information, we forced Bob to reconsider his standard response. Bob receives hundreds of calls asking for his time. Even when a pertinent core value declaration is placed in front of him, he instinctively rejects the meeting. By reminding him through a question that the topic is valuable to him, we opened up the door for a meeting. When he finally agreed to the presentation, we didn't dive into any additional detail or exclaim "That's great!" Instead, we matter-of-factly provided leadership by telling him sufficient minutes was sufficient and closing the call.

These scripts are based on actual scripts that we have written and used in large companies throughout America. In a single week of use, a single member of one company was able to schedule meetings with ten senior-level prospects at major financial services and insurance companies. I have kept a copy of the calendar week as a testimony to the power of this type of cold-calling script.

On Monday, the twenty-first of May, he had a meeting with senior executives at Fidelity Investments. That afternoon, he met with a CIO and a CFO from Merrill Lynch. On Tuesday the twenty-second, he met with the VP of systems architecture from Lehman Brothers. Wednesday the twenty-third, he hosted the chief marketing officer and the chief strategy officer from AIG. On Thursday the twenty-fourth, he had a meeting with the SVP of marketing at Goldman Sachs. Friday, he concluded the week by meeting with a VP of strategic planning at Citicorp and the CFO and director of financial analysis at Aetna.

That particular individual was extremely gifted. When equipped with *The Must-React System*, he became a meeting-scheduling machine. You can achieve similar results with the proper implementation of The System. In most cases, I personally write scripts for my clients. But you can begin by using some of the examples presented above.

How to Write a *Must-React* E-mail

Current e-mail presentations are entirely too product-centric and content heavy. These types of e-mail campaigns typically boast of results in the fractions of a single percent. But because e-mail prospecting is so inexpensive, companies can afford to produce miniscule results. The *Must-React* e-mail typically produces between a 5% and 10% conversion rate. Meaning, if we send one hundred e-mails to prospects, we can expect to schedule meetings with at least five to ten people. At a recent implementation of The System, we recorded an astonishing 19% conversion rate from an e-mail campaign! I have included actual examples from the campaign as the example in this book.

To summarize the campaign, we sent e-mails to one hundred targets. We received sixty-nine total responses from our initial e-mail blast. Out of that sixty-nine, thirty-six indicated no interest in their first response; thirty asked what the e-mail was regarding; and three scheduled a meeting. This was our initial e-mail:

> **From:** _Justin Frosch_
> **To:** _Randy Smith_
> **Sent:** _Monday, July 7, 2003 12:09_ PM
> **Subject:** _con-call mtg_
>
> _Mr. Smith,_
>
> _Our founder and CEO, Mr. Kraig Kleeman, asked me to schedule a conference call with you at your earliest convenience. Do you have availability during the week of July 15? Please advise. Thanks!_
>
> _Kind Regards,_
> _Justin Frosch_
> _Executive Assistant to Chief Executive Officer_
> _Mr. Kraig Kleeman_
> _Blaire Group_
> _p 800.654.7887, ext 307_
> _e justin.frosch@blairegroup.com_
>
> _w www.blairegroup.com_

After receiving our responses, we confirmed the meetings with the three that accepted our initial offer. Then we drafted response e-mails to the thirty-six that indicated they had no interest.

> _Mr. Smith,_
>
> _As part of the project, our analysts conducted simulated sales calls with sales professionals from your company. The results are revealing. Mr. Kleeman would like to share the results of the entire project with you, as well as the results of your team's selling performance. Do you have availability during the week of July 15? Please advise!_

For the thirty-six that responded with no interest and received this e-mail, we saw the following results: fifteen responded to our first round of objection management, four of those fifteen responded no; seven of the fifteen responded requesting more information; and three took a meeting. We drafted a follow up e-mail for the seven that requested more information. Two of the recipients took a meeting. That brought our total to eight meetings successfully scheduled, or an 8% conversion rate. But that wasn't the conclusion.

We also built a response for the thirty that responded to the initial e-mail requesting more information.

> *Mr. Smith,*
>
> *Our founder and CEO, Mr. Kraig Kleeman, is meeting with senior executives from the largest technology companies in North America. His personal research team recently completed its comprehensive research project entitled "Measuring Selling Effectiveness: Technology Sector Companies." As part of the project, our analysts conducted simulated sales calls with more than one thousand technology sales professionals. Mr. Kleeman would like to share the results with you. Do you have availability during the week of July 15? Please advise!*

Nineteen of the thirty responded to our objection management. Five of those declined a meeting. Eight had different excuses for not scheduling a meeting that week but suggested they would meet later in the month. Three of the thirty scheduled a meeting. This brought our total conversion rate to 11%.

When we followed-up on the original thirty-one that never responded to the initial e-mail with phone contact, we were able to schedule an additional eight meetings. That gave us nineteen total scheduled meetings. That's a 19% conversion rate for an e-mail campaign! Out of that nineteen, we had five cancellations. Fourteen of the meetings happened. Four of those meetings turned into qualified opportunities with interest in speaking to our sales force.

By all measures, this is an outstanding campaign. Even by our normal expectations, we were floored at the response. The power of the *Must-React* e-mail is that it removes us from the sales process. It is focused on the core values declaration instead of the product. It is personalized to the prospect. We carefully stylize our subject line on a regular basis. The goal is to avoid looking like the other two hundred e-mails that are being blasted from marketing machines throughout the U.S. We also maintain the principle of Less is More by never including an attachment. Attachments alert prospects to marketing e-mails. No matter how often a prospect may request more information, we advise avoiding a provision attachment until you have had a chance to qualify them.

I advise all of my clients to create a strategy for combining e-mail and voice contact with targets. Prospecting starts with limited-content, personalized e-mailing. Couple that effort with core value, purpose-driven voice contact, and you will create enormous results.

Building a *Must-React* Briefing

In Chapter 4, we discussed the importance of building an environment where the prospect feels safe and will share more information than they will via e-mail or on a cold call. We've also called this safe place the qualification briefing or a *Must-React* briefing. Internally, we call this a qualification briefing. And we understand that it is to be used to motivate the prospect to wholesome dialogue about their project. But externally, we always position this as a research-based briefing. But it is important to understand that these are two names for the same thing. The purpose of this tool is to qualify the need the prospect has for your solution while presenting them relevant industry information built around your core value.

This is a powerful qualification tool. Most sales personnel have been trained to do qualification on their cold calls. When I teach this process to new companies, there are always some who are frustrated that the prospect is not qualified prior to the call. But The System depends on using this briefing to get the prospect to share the most possible information. I have been on calls where prospects will literally tell me their project budget, timeframe, other competitors, and their primary goals. This tool can be used to extract any information that you need to qualify an opportunity.

Many of the studious salespersons I have worked with acknowledge that the best opportunities are often not budgeted projects. The reason for this is that if there is a budget, it is likely that the competition is already involved. If there is an active project, you might be fighting an uphill battle. But many people still do prospecting as if they are looking only for people who have projects. I believe you should have a cross section of both in your pipeline. But traditional prospecting methodologies are based specifically on finding projects. They will often bulldoze those who do not have a defined project. The briefing gives you the ability to "sniff" an opportunity out. You can both discover if there is an active project with budget and timeframe and if there is a genuine need that you can use to build a sales cycle.

The briefing is a PowerPoint presentation of no more than fifteen slides. Each presentation includes an agenda, three major issues, eight fast facts, two case studies, industry analyst best practices, and next steps. A briefing never includes a slide of your company history. It never includes a slide of some of your favorite clients. It certainly *never* includes a slide with a diagram of your product! All of these slides betray the fact that the briefing has been set up as informative and not a sales tool. The moment any of these types of slides are used, the cover is blown. If you show a slide of your favorite customers, you might as well say, "I know we scheduled this as an information briefing, but really, it's a sales pitch. Surprise!" If you do this, it will negate the purpose of making the prospect feel safe and able to communicate with you about interest in your topic.

The communication that happens in this safe place is essential for *The Must-React System*. Because there is often a heavy push to close hard for a meeting during initial prospecting activity, the briefing needs to be used for additional discovery actions that need to be performed. You absolutely need to know where your prospect belongs in the account, what their feelings are on your problem and solution, if they know who signs the checks, who else is involved in the project, etc. The philosophy we are trying to convince you of is that people are going to be likely to share this type of information in a short briefing format than they will on a cold call or over e-mail. The way to begin soliciting this information is through a principle we call Permission-Based Qualifying.

Permission-Based Qualifying is a powerful tool employed at the beginning of the briefing. The principle is simple. When all of your attendees have joined the presentation, you begin by stating that you have shared the information in the presentation several times and it always proves to be helpful. Then you say, "So that I can best serve you during our thirty minutes together, do you mind if I ask you a few questions?" I have never, never, never heard a prospect say no. They are always open to answering almost any question at this point. Often, I will spend ten to twenty minutes of our time on the introduction slide just speaking with the prospects about their project or interest in this matter. You should plan to have up to, but not more than, five questions prepared if the prospect is slow to open up at this point in the presentation. You can use references on later slides to qualify needs and interests. It's all about stimulating the target to wholesome dialogue about his or her particular environment, problems, and needs.

After performing the initial qualification, we say something like, "Thank you for that information. This presentation will be even more relevant to you than I had originally hoped." Then we move on to the agenda slide. I split every presentation into five categories:

- Industry Issues
- Fast Facts
- Case Studies
- Analyst Opinions/Best Practices
- Next Steps

I briefly explain the five sections and then ask for basic agreement on the agenda itself. I also determine if there were any topics the attendees would like to add to the agenda. We don't want to spend very much time on this slide, but we do want to give our audience an idea of where we are going during the presentation.

After the agenda, we move into the "industry issues." There is some flexibility here, but I advise using three issues that all center around the core value declaration used to get the meeting. I built a presentation for a company with an e-mail management product that was titled "Pushing the Envelope: Optimizing E-mail Management." During the presentation, the issues we addressed were:

- Explosive growth of e-mail
- Regulatory compliance requirements and legal discovery
- Lifecycle management standards

As we presented each of the issues, we would ask how they had a bearing on the prospect. This gave us additional qualification data, and it feels conversational.

The next two or three slides of our presentation are built around the eight fast facts. These are short bullets citing relevant data from industry research leaders and consultants. We group these facts around the three issues that we laid out on the second slide. What we are doing during these first three slides is building a case for the problem that we hope to solve. But not only that; we are building the problem in a way that emphasizes our strategy for dealing with it. Think of this as telling a story. The first few slides are the explanation of what is wrong in the world.

We continue to argue that something is wrong in the world by presenting two industry case studies. These can be customers or they can be stories that you have picked up in the news. If they are customers, you don't want to emphasize that at this point in the conversation. Also, the case study slides should only take up two slides. We aren't giving an in-depth description of what happened at these companies, and we certainly don't need to write it all on the slide. We are simply showing that the problem is not just theoretical. It is having an effect on real companies in the real world.

Now we have firmly established that there is a problem. What we want to do next is to show that there is an unbiased strategy being advised by some of the top industry consulting agencies. This is the section we dubbed "analyst opinions/best practices." This isn't our own press; this is the big brains of the industry telling us how this problem needs to be solved. This section can be one or two slides in length.

These slides are the perfect point to get your prospects to open up about their views and strategies for dealing with the problem you have just described. You may find out that they aren't concerned about the problem, but they are being forced to investigate it by their boss, who has a mandate from the CIO. Although your prospect isn't the internal champion you would have hoped, you have discovered that there is conversation on the topic being mandated by a chief officer. That's great information for a discovery phase of the sales cycle. You may also find that they are using the very guidelines that you have presented. Or you may discover that they aren't concerned about all of the issues that the consultants and analysts have come up with, but they are very interested in one or two. These are the types of conversations that are going to help you determine your strategy for next steps with this account.

The beauty of the "best practices" slide is that it maps with your solution. I once presented to the CIO of a fortune 500 company and several of his direct reports. When we reached this slide, I simply asked which of these issues was of highest importance to the CIO. The phone was quiet for a moment. Then we heard the CIO pounding his fist against the table and shouting into the phone, "We need all six of these implemented *immediately!*" If the prospect expresses an interest in that strategy, like the CIO in my story, you have a "softball" of a close for a deeper explanation of your automated solution for dealing with the problem. This is when I move to the final slide, which lists three possible next-step opportunities. At this point, we close for a next step with the prospect. We can regroup and determine a strategy for the account afterward. But we want to make sure that we get the prospect to commit to some sort of continuing action that will keep them in communication with us. We call these continuing actions "definitive next steps." It is critical that you and your team be adequately tightly prepared to lead your prospects to a very specific next step. I helped one large software company create the following definitive next steps:

1. Subject Matter Expert Meeting
2. Deeper Dive Discussion
3. Product Demonstration
4. Proof of Concept Meeting
5. Trial Planning Meeting

It may be that they are going to arrange an opportunity for us to present the same presentation to a larger group in their company. They may be interested in viewing a demonstration of our product. Whatever the next step is, schedule it at the end of your meeting. The prospect is very busy. As kind as their intentions might be, they may never actually call back like they promise. You need to use the time that they have devoted to you and schedule the next step.

Hopefully, you are beginning to understand how the principles of The System can help you build your prospecting collateral. *The Must-React System* is designed to increase the productivity of all of your prospecting efforts.

Conclusion

Although prospecting is broken in most sales organizations, we have a vision for how it should work. *The Must-React System* has been designed to give the modern salesperson the tools he or she needs to attract new business opportunities in existing and net-new accounts. The System is industry agnostic. It has been used to contact heads of state and to sell companies. It has built tens of millions of dollars in net-new pipeline for a software company, and it has grown young companies into lucrative competitors. All of these successes are tied to the simple truths laid out in our System's principles.

There's no secret behind what we've told you throughout this book. The power to achieve success through this system will depend on your ability to let go of old bad habits and to embrace the new prospecting model.

Too many salespersons have given up on prospecting. We all know that it has been painful to pick up the phone from time to time. But with *The Must-React System*, you will be able to secure meaningful discussions with your contacts.

Remember, prospecting is both art and science. The principles of The System need to be adjusted to fit your sales organization. But once you learn to use them to your advantage, I am sure that you will keep them in your sales toolkit for the rest of your career. Students of mine who began in entry-level marketing and sales positions just two years ago have graduated to making very handsome six-figure incomes. When I cross paths with them, they always tell me that they are continuing to employ the principles of The System that I used to train them. We often shake our heads about their colleges, who are stuck in the old useless methodologies of prospecting.

I have done my best to give examples of how The System works in a cold-calling script, an e-mail campaign, and a presentation. Building core values and these strategies with The System principles in mind can be very daunting if you have never received personalized training. Often, I will help a client build several scripts, presentations, and e-mails. Afterward, they are able to duplicate the efforts. But normally, it takes several days of workshops before the lights truly go on.

Prospecting is my passion and it is my gift. I speak with many chief marketing and sales officers who are frustrated with their current demand-creation processes. I believe their frustrations are justified because they have tried so many quick fixes that have failed to produce lasting results. Fortunately, The System is designed to approach prospecting holistically from the top down. We are able to produce marketing strategies, tracking systems and metrics, and even marketing collateral designed to employ the principles associated with The System. Through these practices, marketing officers will be able to tie themselves to revenue. And sales executives will be able to accurately manage their demand-creation process.

It is my hope that this book has been a launching pad for your company to accelerate productivity in the realm of lead generation, demand creation, and personal persuasion.

APPENDIX A

Self-Evaluation

Self-examination is powerful. When I conduct *Must-React* seminars across the globe, I typically begin by asking attendees to complete a Cold-Calling Self-Assessment Survey. Then, as a class, we discuss everyone's current approach. In a warm, yet truthful way, I explain why most of them fail. Before digging deeper into the pages of this book, I encourage you to experience the same exercise by completing the forms below.

Scenario #1
Target: _____
Objective: Qualify for opportunity and gain initial meeting
Answerer: Administrative Assistant

Please write your cold call presentation below. Please be sure to include the dialogue as if the admin answers the call.

Admin: Mr. Bob Williams' office. May I help you?

Your Words:

Admin:

Your Words:

Admin:

Your Words:

Scenario #2

Target: _____
Objective: Qualify for opportunity and gain initial meeting
Answerer: Target

Please write your cold-call presentation below.

Please be sure to include the dialogue as if the target answers the call.

Target:　　　　Hello, this is Bob Williams.
Your Words:

Target:

Your Words:

Target:

Your Words:

Objections Management

- Who is (your company)?
-
-

- What is this regarding?
-
-

- Are you selling any type of software, hardware, or consulting services?
-
-

- Is this a sales call?
-
-

- Does Mr. X know you or your company?
-
-

- Can you please send me an e-mail describing your request?
-
-

APPENDIX B

Third-Party Evaluation

Most companies readily institute a comprehensive financial audit to ensure strict adherence to company policy, as well as to provide a deep system of stringent fiscal accountability. An uncompromising commitment to this practice strengthens shareholder confidence by creating an environment of suitable integrity. In the same spirit of insisting on accountability and integrity, why not audit your sales team?

Your sales team is the cornerstone of your business. It represents the front line for communicating your offerings and value propositions to your prospect and customer base. It is an undeniable fact that sales representatives can easily make or break the opinion of your company in the competitive marketplace. The sales process is fragile. When relying on human execution, the potential for error is great. How does your sales team operate? What do they say? You have revenue figures, but do you really know the content of the message that they carry? More than likely, they have undergone extensive training, but are they utilizing the proper techniques to advance and close deals? Even if your company is prosperous, it is possible that there is a large gap between the perceived success of your sales team members and the reality of their missed potential.

What is a Sales-Audit?

Similar to a financial audit, a Sales-Audit provides an across-the-board assessment of the relative strengths and weaknesses for both individual sales professionals and entire sales teams. A Sales-Audit helps companies identify both positive and negative trends. The results deliver powerful information that assist with customizing future sales training efforts by targeting critical areas. Your management team will be presented performance in the form of quantitative and qualitative results.

An unaudited sales team results in:

- unmet sales objectives,
- loss of client opportunities due to ineffective technique,
- a confused customer base due to non-uniform messaging,
- and missed revenue targets due to poor execution.

A Sales-Audit provides a weighted, quantitative scorecard analyzing each sales representative's relative performance regarding pivotal sales-technique metrics. Additionally, a summary-weighted scorecard is provided to illustrate trends and effectiveness for the entire sales team.

How do Your Customers and Prospects Perceive Your Sales Teams?

Marketing executives routinely "listen in" on customer service representatives' calls with customers. It is an accepted practice that produces powerful knowledge. Imagine the power of knowing what your sales professionals are really saying to your clients and prospects. By conducting a Sales-Audit, you'll get detailed answers to the following questions:

- Is your sales team communicating the correct message?
- Do your sales professionals convey products and services effectively?
- Do they employ professionalism regarding basic actions like rapid follow-up or probing for a deeper understanding of your prospect's pain points? Are they adequately articulating the vision of your company and its solutions?

- Is your sales team capable of engaging prospects in intelligent, requisite dialogue that naturally leads to properly defined next steps?
- Do they speak in terms of benefits or features?
- Are their presentations overly technology-driven and potentially unintelligible to the laymen?
- How does your sales team perform in the critical area of prospect development?
- How do they compare against sales representatives from your competitors?

A Sales-Audit will bring resolution to these unsolved mysteries.

How is the Sales-Audit Scorecard Organized?

The scorecard is presented in three formats:

- Sales Member Scorecard: Each sales professional audited is presented with a scorecard reflecting his or her individual audit.
- Sales Team Scorecard: This is a trend analysis documenting collective performance for the team.
- Competitive Analysis Scorecard: This provides documented results from your sales team's audit evaluated alongside your selected competitors' audit.

Each scorecard is fully customizable and organized into the following nine sections:

1. **Core Message Presentation:** This section examines the accuracy and clarity of the presentation of your corporate history, company philosophy, and core competencies as expressed by your sales team. Errors in fundamental

messaging skills can be fatal to any selling process and must be corrected immediately.

2. **Essential Communication:** A thorough examination of necessary communications skills is conducted for each member of your sales team. As an example, research indicates that vocal tone boosts communication effectiveness by 80%.[9] Sales teams who have not mastered vocal intonation skills are regarded as poor communicators.

3. **Competitive Intelligence:** Do your sales professionals probe to determine which of your competitors are contending for the business? Do they accurately evaluate the stage of competitor involvement? Failure to thoroughly understand a possible competitive stronghold can mean a tremendous waste of valuable company time and resources.

4. **Qualifying Inquiry:** This section analyzes appropriate qualifying skills. Does your sales team qualify appropriately? Studies show that top sales producers win as the result of having mastered superior qualification techniques.

5. **Product Knowledge:** A complete examination of product knowledge and product messaging is conducted. Do members of your sales team thoroughly understand the prospect's challenges? Do they recommend appropriate solutions? Failure to do so can result in prospects that do not put confidence in your company.

6. **Use of Persuasive Resources:** Do your sales professionals leverage helpful, persuasive resources? For example: Guiding the prospect to your home page and performing a simple demonstration could ignite interest and accelerate next-step action items. A lack of resourcefulness may undermine credibility.

7. **Closing:** Closing a deal is a natural step in a cycle that is comprised of a series of closes. Do your sales team members understand that every meeting should conclude with some type of close? For example: A "next-step" road map should be identified at the close of every juncture. Each meeting

is simply a fulfillment of previously agreed-upon objectives that graduate to the next step.

8. **Professionalism:** This section answers basic questions about each sales professional. Do your sales professionals exhibit professional behavior? Are they helpful and courteous? Do they exude confidence and motivate prospects to conduct business with your firm?

9. **Subjective Commentary:** This is a value-added section in which the analyst has the ability to express findings in paragraph format that might not be reflected in the audit data.

How is the Data Tabulated?

After conducting each audit, your analyst completes individual scorecards and ultimately calculates the entire group's performance, which highlights trends. Your analyst will additionally gather competitive data to provide an assessment of your team's performance compared against your selected peer and competitor group.

For each sales team member, the Sales-Audit results will reveal strengths and weaknesses by category.

What are Weighted Values?

Scores are carefully determined by using The Blaire Group's Sales-Audit Weighted Value System ^{SM} for factors that you deem most important. Fully customizable weights are multipliers that provide scoring intended to mirror your corporate priorities. For example, weights of 10, 20, and 30 can be selected based on the following criteria:

10 = Significant
20 = Vital
30 = Critical

What Does the Scale Mean?

When evaluating your sales team, performance will be ranked by the following guidelines:

0 = Failed execution, no attempt made
1 = Made attempt, but not convincing
2 = Demonstrated competence
3 = Excellent, perfect execution

Summary Evaluation

When the percentiles have been formulated and the sales team has been ranked, your analyst will evaluate both individual and overall team performances. Your management team will be presented performance in the form of quantitative and qualitative results. The Blaire Group shares your high standards. Our percentile rankings are as follows:

90 to 100 Percentile–Exceeds expectations
80 to 90 Percentile–Meets expectations
Below 80 Percentile–Fails to meet expectations

"New prospect meeting and acquisition execution score for multiple industries was 50%, far below the Zone of Acceptance, which is 80%. Organizations that have been trained in *The Must-React System*, however, scored 94% for new prospect meeting and acquisition execution. When surveyed, users of *The Must-React System* cite revised call scripts and the ability to execute research based briefings as the two components of The System most responsible for the increases in effectiveness."[10]

Essential Communication	Weight	Scale	Score
Punctuality (response time)	10	3	30
Response to direct inquiry	10	3	30
Effective listening	30	3	90
Open-ended questioning	30	3	90
Objection management	20	3	60
Presentation effectiveness	30	3	90
Use of examples, case studies	10	3	30
Tone	10	3	30
Enunciation	10	3	30
Grammar	10	3	30
Maintaining focus	10	3	30
Probe for pain points	10	3	30
	Competency Score		570
	Max Section Total		570
	Score (%)		100%

Qualifying Inquiry	Weight	Scale	Score
Political map	20	0	0
Opportunity identification	30	3	90
Budget	20	1	20
Timeframe	20	1	20
Decision maker and contact info	20	1	20
Activity requirements to close	20	0	0
	Competency Score		150
	Max Section Total		390
	Score (%)		38%

Competitive Intelligence	Weight	Scale	Score
Competitor evaluation	10	1	10
Initial inquiry	10	3	30
Activity history	10	0	0
Current state	10	0	0
	Competency Score		40
	Max Section Total		120
	Score (%)		33%

Core Message Presentation	Weight	Scale	Score
Corporate history	10	3	30
Company philosophy	30	3	90
Core competencies	10	2	20
Effectiveness/persuasiveness	30	3	90
Competency Score			230
Max Section Total			240
Score (%)			96%

Product Knowledge	Weight	Scale	Score
WMS concepts & issues	30	3	90
Prescribed steps	30	3	90
Demonstrated credibility	30	3	90
Competency Score			270
Max Section Total			270
Score (%)			100%

Use of Persuasive Resources	Weight	Scale	Score
Requirements meeting	10	3	30
Next steps	10	3	30
Forward relevant information	10	3	30
Competency Score			90
Max Section Total			90
Score (%)			100%

Closing	Weight	Scale	Score
Create sense of urgency	10	1	10
Next step consensus	30	3	90
Competency Score			100
Max Section Total			120
Score (%)			83%

Professionalism	Weight	Scale	Score
Helpful attitude/courteous	30	3	90
Exhibit confidence	30	3	90
Exhibit credibility	30	3	90
	Competency Score		270
	Max Section Total		270
	Score (%)		100%

Composite Results			Score
	Grand Total		1720
	Max Audit Total		2070
	Total Audit Score (%)		83%

Endnotes

1. Rumbaska, Frank, "Never Cold Call Again," http://www.dontcoldcall.com/products.htm, paragraph 2.
2. Galper, Ari, "Unlock the Game: Cold Calling Doesn't Have to be Painful," http://www.unlockthegame.com.
3. "Tips for Successful Cold Calling," All Business, http://www.allbusiness.com/sales/selling-techniques-telesales/1355-1.html.
4. Sanford, Mark, "Rules for Maximizing Call Effectiveness,"http://www.coldcalling.com.
5. Direct Marketing Association, *Direct Marketing Statistics and Yields* (New York, 2007). 24.
6. Blaire Group, *Pipeline Predictability* (Chicago, 2008). 8.
7. Blaire Group, *Pipeline Predictability* (Chicago, 2008). 12.
8. Blaire Group, *Measuring Selling Effectiveness* (Chicago, 2008 abridged). 28.
9. Blaire Group Research, *Certification Survey* (Chicago, 2007). 18-22.
10. Baire Group Research, *Certification Survey* (Chicago, 2007). 23-27.

About the Author

Kraig Kleeman has overseen more than one million cold-call presentations in his career. He developed *The Must-React System*^{SM}, which equips sales professionals to achieve mastery in the area of sales talk-time. *The Must-React System* contains critical selling competencies that are vital for cold calling, prospecting, pipeline development, and simple introductory messaging to targeted buyers. Mr. Kleeman's knowledge and expertise includes twenty-plus years' experience in sales and business development. His primary areas of core development are cold calling and sales-pipeline development strategies. He was founder and CEO of Express Direct. Under his leadership, Express Direct grew from $0 to $20 million in sales in less than four years. The growth of Express Direct was directly related to the sales efficiencies and methodologies that he developed at that time. After the successful sale of Express Direct to a West Coast technology firm, Mr. Kleeman was retained by various corporations for assistance with lead-generation programs, sales team assessment/development support, and sales pipeline expansion consulting. He has commercialized *The Must-React System*. His consulting organization, Blaire Group, is named after his daughter Blaire. Mr. Kleeman regularly engages in consulting projects designed to identify selling flaws and bring correction, public speaking, and sales coaching. Inquiries can be made at www.blairegroup.com.

Made in the USA
Lexington, KY
21 March 2013